MW00626787

HOW TO DESIGN YOUR PERFECT INTERIOR

(AND MAINTAIN YOUR SANITY AND BUDGET)

by Gail Doby, ASID

Cover image courtesy of Jamie Drake, FASID - Showhouse Beverly Hills, CA
Photographer for Cover Image - Art Gray

Copyright © 2012 Design Success University Press
© 2012 American Society of Interior Designers
ISBN: 9780615770246
All rights reserved. No part of this publication may be reproduced or transmitted in any form
or by any means, electronic, or mechanical, including photocopying, recording, or by any
information storage and retrieval system

TABLE OF CONTENTS

Preface 10

Acknowledgments 19

Legal Disclaimer 20

Chapter 1 21
Where Do You Start? 21
Start with Your "Why" 22
What Does Home Mean to You? 23
Exercise #1 24

Chapter 2 25
How Do Your Values and Priorities Affect Your Design Project? 25
Time and Money 26
Brand Promises and Their Effect on Your Decisions 27
Trends, Brands and Their Influence 28
Where to Get Design Ideas 29
Exercise #2 30

Chapter 3 33
The Design Process 33
Where to Shop 34
Design Process: Programming 34
Design Process: Conceptual Design and Schematics 36
Design Process: Design Development 36
Design Process: Contract Documents and Specifications 38
Installation 39
Job Finalization 39

Chapter 4 41
What Is Your Home Currently Like? 41
Your Bathroom's Safety and Function Are as Important as Its Beauty 42
Exercise #3 44

Chapter 5   **45**

Good Design - Why It Matters and Considerations That Impact Your

Decisions   45

Good Design: Kitchens   46

Good Design: Bathrooms   47

Good Design: Bedrooms   49

Good Design: Family and Great Rooms   51

Additional "Good Design" Considerations   52

Good Design: Lighting and Technology   53

Good Design: Health and Safety   54

Good Design: Air Quality   56

Good Design: Durability   56

Good Design: Ergonomics   57

Good Design: Conservation and Green Design   57

Chapter 6   **59**

Prioritizing Your Investment   59

Financial Decisions and the Economy   61

Design vs. Decorating   62

Remodeling and Construction Design   64

Chapter 7   **67**

Common and Costly Mistakes to Avoid   67

Scale   68

Proportion   69

Durability   71

Appropriate Finishes and Materials   72

Buying Online   72

Budget Dilemmas   73

Chapter 8   **75**

Can I Really Do This Project Myself, and More Importantly, Do I

Want to Do It Myself?   75

Chapter 9   **79**

How to Accomplish Your Interior Design Projects Do-It-Yourself vs.

Hiring a Professional   79

Do-It-Yourself   80
Design Advice + Do-It-Yourself   80
Online Designers   81
Full-Service Interior Design Firms   82
Top Tier Designers   91

Chapter 10   **94**
Planning Your Project – Do Your Homework   94
Tools   95
Evaluate Professionally Executed Projects   95
Document Your Room or Project   96
Analyze Your Current Furnishings   97
Create a Drawing of Your Space   98
Create Your Wish List   100
Select Your Palette   100
Select Your Furnishings   102
Rugs   102
Art   103
Window Treatments   104
Accessories   106

Chapter 11   **108**
How to Find and Choose a Design Professional   108
Now That You Understand the Design Process...   109
No-Fee Designers   110
When You Need an Architect   111
When You Need a Contractor or Builder   112
Licensing Requirements   113
Who Do You Hire First?   115
Where Do You Find an Interior Designer?   116
How Do Designers Charge?   122
References   127
Insurance   128
Contracts or Letters of Agreement   129
When Things Go Wrong ... and They Do   131
You Change Your Mind   132
Your Designer Doesn't Listen to You or Does Something You

Don't Like 132
Your Travel, Personal or Business Schedule Is Excessively
Demanding 132
You Are Anxious About Your Decisions 133
If You and Your Partner Don't Agree 133
If You Are Indecisive 133
Communication 134
Unmet Expectations 135

Chapter 12 **136**
How Much Does It Cost? 136
How to Set Your Budget 137
What Should I Expect to Pay a Designer? 143
How to Manage Your Budget 143
When Does "Saving Money" By Doing It Yourself Really Cost You
Money? 145

Chapter 13 **146**
The Process of Design 146
What to Expect 147
How Long Does It Take? 147
What Happens When Something Goes Wrong? 149
What Are My Responsibilities When I Work With a Design
Professional? 150

Chapter 14 **152**
How to Relax and Enjoy the Process 152
Tips to Survive a Remodel 153
Realistic Deadlines 153
Phobias and Irritations 154
Security 155
Set Up Temporary Spaces So Your Family Can Function 156
Construction Hours and Noise 157
Staging of Tools and Materials 157
Contractor Etiquette 157
Communication Is Crucial 158
How to Keep Your Crew Happy 158

Keep Your Neighbors Happy   159
Keep Pets and Children Away From the Project   160
Timing   161
Budget Control   162
"While You're At It..."   162
Change Orders   163

Chapter 15   **164**
Looking Forward   164

Chapter 16   **166**
About ASID and DSU   166
What ASID Appellations Mean   168
Design Success University   169

Chapter 17   **170**
Resources and Sponsors   170
Acronyms/Glossary   171
Design Apps   173

TESTIMONIALS

"Whether we work on our own or with the help of a design professional this book will serve as an invaluable aid. It dispels certain myths about interior design while shining a light on the services designers provide; services that make our interiors functional and safe as well as inviting. *How to Design Your Perfect Interior* is a must for those seeking beauty in their homes,"

Barbara Barry, interior designer & author of *Around Beauty*

"This is an invaluable comprehensive guide for both interior designers and consumers. Potentially, this could change the landscape of client relationships in the world of interior design. I can't wait to use this tool in my business. A 'must have' for anyone embarking on a building, decorating or remodeling project,"

Kristin Drohan, interior designer and furniture designer
http://www.kristindrohancollection.com/

"For the home design enthusiast: *How to Design Your Perfect Interior* clearly explains what is involved with an interior design project before you invest a lot of your hard-earned time and money. Reading this book will prevent costly and stressful mistakes. Whether you want to do your project yourself, or you want to work with a design professional, this book gives you tips and suggestions to achieve the home of your dreams.

For interior designers: The book you've always wished for is finally here! *How to Design Your Perfect Interior* explains the complexities and costs of the interior design process to potential consumers of design services. Once the reader understands how designers can save time and money because of their unique talent, forethought, problem solving abilities, education, experience, persistence, management skills, and passion, they can make an informed decision about doing the project themselves or hiring a design professional. I look forward to sharing this with my clients because they will know how to be a great client, why we as designers are worth the investment and how to communicate effectively"

Susan Hopkins, ASID, interior designer

"This book has information that anyone considering an interior design project should study and use as a reference. And it's not just for someone who's a "DIY-er." As a design professional, I truly like having these many elements separated and defined. It can only streamline an effective project, engage conversations and clarify terms for designer and client. The information about the construction phase is a wonderful reminder!"

Clare H, Golan, ASID, interior designer and "Design Sense" blogger

PREFACE

"Your house is not a home until it expresses your soul." – Gail Doby

Stephen Pararo, ASID/Photos courtesy of Pineapple House Interior Design

Is great design a luxury that only the privileged few can enjoy? If it were, then national stores like Bed, Bath and Beyond® would not ask designers and architects with recognizable "brand names" like Barbara Barry to design beautiful bed linens for the masses.

What Is Design?

Design uses analytical and intuitive skills to understand our emotional motivations, desires and practical needs. Design is also about applying knowledge of materials and processes, and looking for creative ways to solve problems that did not previously exist. Design is about searching for ways to customize, enhance and improve the functionality, as well as the user's experience, of something that currently exists.

Design is omnipresent, visible, invisible and life-enhancing.

Practical design makes your life more efficient and organized, and can even impact your health. For example, some products emit harmful chemicals or odors and others may give off microscopic fibers that can degrade indoor air quality. With good design your home is safer when these products are avoided.

Great design elegantly solves problems and is aesthetically pleasing at the same time.

Inspiring design evokes emotions that add to the enjoyment and experience of your surroundings. It contributes to your sense of well-being and happiness.

When design is done to perfection, you feel and sense it without it overpowering what really matters—the people who use and enjoy the spaces.

Design can even make you smile with appreciation and delight or bring tears to your eyes.

DESIGN IS AN OUTWARD REFLECTION OF YOUR INTERNAL MOTIVATIONS

Your home is the ultimate expression of your personality, values, emotions, taste and priorities.

Economically challenging times affect our sense of security, and especially during these times, your home is your haven. It is the place you feel safe, relaxed and connected to those closest to you and protected from the world outside.

Since you spend the majority of every day in your home, you deserve to love it.

For many of us, our home gives us great satisfaction, a feeling of pride and the thrill of accomplishment because we can create, invest in and enjoy a few special items that we maybe couldn't afford as college students and young couples.

Perhaps you want to feel proud of designing your own interior, so you should do it yourself.

Or, maybe you want some services from a professional, but you want to do most of the work. There are designers that will help you with the concepts, shop with you and review your selections.

Alternately, you may want someone to do most of the work for you and manage the process, but you need to do it in phases because you don't want to borrow the money that it would take to do it all at once. That is also a good option. Just be open and honest with the designer or decorator if you plan to do the work in phases.

Finally, for some, having a beautiful home created by a top-tier designer is an expression of their success and appreciation for items uniquely crafted for them and no one else. Purchasing at chain retail stores is not the option they choose because they will see the same thing in other homes. Those patrons support artistic expression that few can afford. They value their time and appreciate the creativity and services of others so they can enjoy the result without being concerned with the process.

WHY WE WROTE THIS BOOK

Because you care enough about the role of design in your life to read this book, we can assume you want to "live beautifully." We wrote this book to help you achieve your personal goals with your interior design project.

We also wrote this book to "pull back the curtain" on the role of interior designers and provide insights into a complex process that is a combination of artistry, intense planning, a multitude of details, careful project management and "cat-herding" (how interior designers often feel when we manage all of the people and details).

Designers see things differently than most people. We challenge conventional thinking when we design and carefully edit those concepts, create drawings and sketches, assemble swatches, color chips and samples. We also learn about construction, codes, electrical, plumbing, and many more technical skills to accomplish the final result. We visualize complete projects in our heads before the contractor or builder starts the job.

We solve many problems along the way because problems do inevitably happen. We open a wall and find that a pipe prevents us from locating a plumbing fixture where we drew it in the plans. We have to punt. Experience and teamwork help to solve those challenges.

It also takes years to find the right resources and team members to make your vision become tangible. It is what designers do every day, and if we do it right, it seems effortless and magical. It isn't.

Years ago, so the story goes, a designer was asked to consult on a design problem for a commercial space, and he gave his advice within minutes.
The designer billed the client $20,000 for his services. When the client asked why he was billed so much for a short conversation, he replied, "It took me 20 years of experience to answer your question." (Possibly this anecdote is based on a famous Picasso story where a woman recognized him in a restaurant and asked him to do a drawing of her on a napkin,

which he did, and then charged her an insane amount. She asked him, "Why such a fee; it only took you a minute?" He answered, "Madam, it took me a lifetime.")

If you work with an interior design professional, and he or she is masterful, one day you share your dreams and visions, then weeks or months later after your designer has spent countless hours following up on orders, meeting with vendors and subcontractors, making sure every single thing is executed according to the plans and solving hundreds of problems, your home goes from ho-hum to awe-inspiring.

Speaking from over 25 years of design experience, I can assure you that interior design is much more stressful, time-consuming and challenging than it appears. Many things happen for your project between the meetings, phone calls and emails. It's like seeing a duck glide on the water when it is madly paddling beneath the surface.

Designers work hard to make it look easy.

Designers become totally engrossed and committed to helping you achieve your vision from the minute they first meet with you. It is not unusual for your designer to wake up in the middle of the night with the "Oh no's!" and "Did I do's?"

Designers want you to be thrilled with your home. It is the ultimate reward for our hard work when we see your delight and tears of joy.

Our goal with this book is to dispel myths and mysteries about design, and to help you avoid costly problems whether you choose to do it yourself or hire a professional.

We will share several short stories throughout this book that illustrate the intricacies of creating your perfect interior. The first story caused more than a few gray hairs and sleepless nights for me.

Ariana Smetana, Student ASID

THE "FRESHEN-UP" PROJECT GONE WILD

A few years ago, a commercial architect friend and neighbor hired my firm for a $25,000 "freshen-up" of his home. Because he wanted to maintain marital harmony, he knew that he could, but shouldn't, design and manage his own residential project. He and his wife had seen several of my projects, and they felt comfortable that I could help them compromise and make decisions quickly.

That seemingly simple project grew with numerous "while you're at it's" into a major $250,000 remodel, including a complete gut of the master suite, addition of a sound system inside and outside, staircase and railings, paint inside and outside, light fixtures inside and outside, windows, doors, skylight, floor refinishing, carpet, new trim and crown molding, hardware, tile backsplash, new furniture, window treatments, accessories and fireplace surround. The three-month deadline didn't change, but the scope increased significantly.

Within a month of starting, the (literally) split-personality contractor walked off the job, and my company had to complete the project. Skylights, windows and doors were partially installed, and at the last-minute, we had to find subcontractors to finish the massive project. The wife was in tears, and we spent a good bit of time consoling her and reassuring her that we would finish the job on time even though we wondered how we'd accomplish it.

It was a feat of will and determination because the painters, trim carpenters and drywall finishers were working at the same time. (Think about dust and paint mixing.) It was a delicate dance to keep the crews working productively.

My business partner, Erin, was getting married within days of the project completion, and her last day of work before her wedding was also the day we installed a carload of accessories. We finished the project at 8 p.m. the night before the architect and his wife left for a European home-exchange.

The architect friend and his wife were thrilled—and exhausted—from the stress of making sure the house was beautiful. Their care and concern about their guests' comfort was not equally rewarded. When they arrived at their guests' home in England, the plumbing was not working in one of the bathrooms.

This story illustrates what can happen even if you are in the industry and know what it takes to manage a massive remodel. The deadline was way too short for the "while you are at it" scope creep and should have taken six to seven months.

UNREAL REALITY TV

If you like watching reality TV design shows, don't be misled by the budget, time frames or processes. Designers groan when they see shows with $2,000 budgets that "only take two days" because they set unrealistic expectations.

The reality shows receive donations for products and services in exchange for visibility. They also have a team of professionals orchestrating the remodels before the show is filmed.

If you were to pay all of the trades, including carpenters, electricians, plumbers, drapery workrooms, tile installers and designers that donate their time for the opportunity, it would cost tens of thousands of dollars, and months of planning to achieve that same result for your project.

Designers' creativity is their intellectual property, so also don't expect three designers to give you their ideas for free like another popular "reality" TV show.

These shows are entertaining but don't accurately reflect reality.

CAN YOU DO IT YOURSELF?

Can you create an interior like you see on TV for yourself? Of course you can. Assuming you have some creative talent and a desire to create your own masterpiece, you can learn how to do it.

Since it takes designers years to learn how to do it, you will encounter challenges, so don't expect that one book will make you an instant expert However, this book will accelerate the process.

FINALLY ...

Because we love design and can't imagine life without it, we wrote this book in the hope of making it easier for you to fall in love with design, too. And when we thought about how to help make that happen, we felt it all started in one place: Organizing your thoughts, which is where we begin when we work with you.

Whether you plan to tackle your own project; get a little design advice from friends, neighbors or online resources; or even hire a professional interior designer to navigate the hundreds or thousands of decisions you will make, preparation is vital. We have included several questionnaires and checklists to help you make wise and educated decisions.

Congratulations on your new design adventure. We sincerely hope you enjoy the result.

Enjoy!

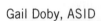

Gail Doby, ASID

Chief Vision Officer & Co-founder of Design Success University
The professional interior designer's business and marketing resource

ACKNOWLEDGEMENTS

Michael Berens, Former Director of Research at ASID, and I spent hours discussing the myths and mysteries about interior design and the practitioner's role in assisting you. We decided to write a book to demystify interior design and dispel the misperceptions about interior designers and what we can do to make the process easy and fun.

You are an intelligent consumer, and we decided that if we could help you be prepared and knowledgeable about the process of design, you could make a more informed decision about this significant investment in your home. As you'll see, it is more than just the financial decision, it involves many emotional decisions as well, and once emotions become involved, how you experience the process and results will be affected.

Thank you to our team of talented editors and contributors including Michael Berens, Harry Doby (my patient husband) and Nancy Greystone, a true "clarifier" that helped express my thoughts more gracefully.

Our graphics team made the book come to life with their creativity including:

Kelly Nelson, Vice President of Marketing and Communications
Jennifer Lipner, Managing Senior Editor
Janine Greene, Marketing Project Associate
Danielle Theroux, Graphic Design Associate

Thank you also to the Design Success University team, including Sarah Schupbach, assistant, and Erin Weir, co-founder and strategic vision director. Without your help and support, I could not have taken the time to write this book.

Claire Golan, Faith Sheridan, Janelle Steinberg, and Drue Lawlor reviewed the book from the interior designer's perspective. We appreciate their feedback and suggestions.

LEGAL DISCLAIMER

Every effort has been made to accurately represent how interior designers work and charge based on the annual Interior Design Fee & Salary Survey that Design Success University conducts. Each interior designer works differently, so this book is meant for educational purposes, and should only be considered a guideline for your project.

If you decide to hire an interior designer, please discuss their fees and your budget with them and ask to see a copy of their contract prior to engaging them for your project.

Design Success University, LLC

2100 North Ursula Street
Suite 424
Aurora, CO 80045

Visit us at http://www.DesignSuccessU.com
dream@howtodesignyourperfectinterior.com

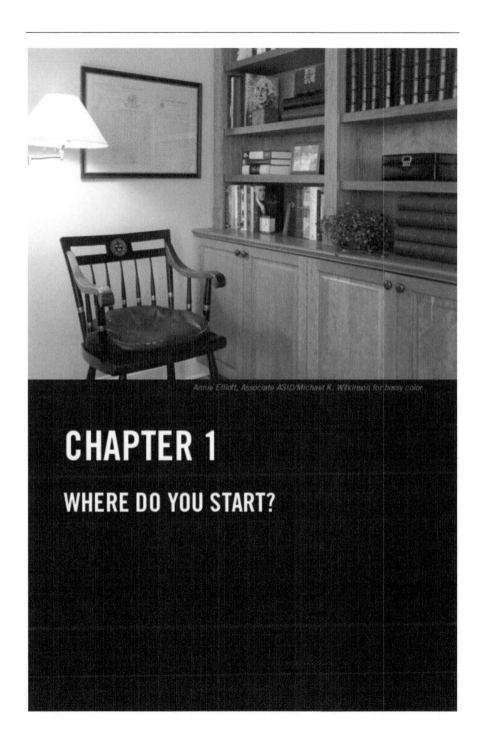

Annie Elliott, Associate ASID/Michael K. Wilkinson for bossy color

CHAPTER 1

WHERE DO YOU START?

Tere Bresin, ASID, CID/Marisa Pellegrini, Photographer

"Design is a necessity, not a luxury. It expresses your personality, makes your life more functional and enhances your enjoyment of life." – Gail Doby

START WITH YOUR "WHY"

Why does design matter to you? It makes your life easier, more gratifying and more beautiful. Great design is about function, form and aesthetics, and it impacts us emotionally.

Design touches every aspect of your life.

You present a personal design statement whether you realize it or not. It is a true reflection of who you are and what you value about yourself, your family and your community.

Therefore, it really does matter what you think and say to yourself when you make decisions about your household investments. Regardless of whether other people's thoughts and opinions matter a little to you or a lot, what matters most—or what *hopefully* matters most—is that you are comfortable in your own home.

The role of interior design in your life is more important than ever. Even if we never invite anyone but our closest friends and family into our inner sanctum, it still affects our personal self-esteem and self-worth.

Good design is more than the aesthetics of furniture, fabrics, colors, art and accessories—even though that is the most visual part of it. Even if you just love beautiful surroundings, you deserve to enjoy what you use and see in your home every day.

If you engage an interior designer, the first step of the process is to understand your motivations for your project as well as your likes, dislikes, priorities, scope of work, budget, goals and deadlines. This is called Programming. It is important to take time for this part of the process, especially if you want to do the work by yourself because it prevents costly mistakes.

We walk you through the process in this book. If you start the project and get overwhelmed, you can always call a professional later. You will be better prepared and more informed than most consumers that ask for assistance.

My favorite design professor also said that we should start each day with our very best silver, china and crystal because we deserve it. Why save it for special occasions? He has a valid point.

WHAT DOES HOME MEAN TO YOU?

How do you feel about your home, and how did your childhood home impact how you live now?

One client's father collected contemporary art and invested in mid-century modern furniture. He was also an engineer, so my client learned about perfection in design and function. Her mother was active in the community, so it was important to have a home she was proud of when she hosted meetings for her charitable activities.

My client's design decisions were strongly influenced by her parents' taste and values.

Exercise #1

- Take a few minutes and write down what you liked and didn't like about your childhood home.
- What were your parent's priorities for your childhood home?
- Without looking at pictures, can you visualize the textures and colors you liked?
- What do you want to incorporate or avoid in your current home?
- Is your home a current reflection of your sense of style, and if not, how would you like to change it?

Annie Elliott, Associate ASID/Michael K. Wilkinson for bossy color

CHAPTER 2

HOW DO YOUR VALUES AND PRIORITIES AFFECT YOUR DESIGN PROJECT?

Your personal values are reflected in every decision you make in your life ... including your home. Whether it matters to you or not, when visitors see your home for the first time, they form instant opinions about you and what is meaningful in your life.

When you feel good about your home, you feel good about yourself.

TIME AND MONEY

How you invest your valuable assets of time and money involves layers of choices and decisions. Since your time is valuable, be sure to factor that into the real cost of your project.

If you are a busy executive working more than 50 hours per week, and your company pays you $50,000, $100,000, $250,000 or more per year, what is the value of your non-working, non-sleeping time?

If your job is to manage a busy household, and raise your children to be productive, healthy and successful, how will it affect your family if you are 100% in charge of your own interior design project?

You will take time from work, children's activities or relaxation to search for bargains and options online, schedule and manage your project. It is a trade-off, and it may sound like a fun and rewarding challenge, or it may be a necessity because a designer's fees for doing the project for you may take dollars away from your furnishings budget.

When you do have free time, how do you want to spend it?

The time and money you spend on your home and interior may result in other trade-offs, like postponing the purchase of a new car or a family vacation.

Is budget one of your most important considerations? Maybe you have a growing family and you are in your twenties. Perhaps you need to stretch. every dollar because you know that when your toddler trips, the sippy cup's lid might unleash a colorful juice on the upholstery, so investing in an expensive sofa with a cotton fabric isn't practical; Perhaps a leather sofa makes the most sense for your current lifestyle. However, if you have pets that lie on your leather sofa, it can get easily scratched, so a darker, durable fabric may be a better option for you. Design decisions involve much more than budget.

If your children are grown and you are ready to develop your "adult" home based on your new lifestyle, does quality play a more important part in your decisions? Is time precious because your work and social life demand the majority of your waking hours? If so, you may want help with your home design, and hiring a professional to assist you may be worth the investment.

As you consider your priorities, values and resources, it can be confusing and sometimes daunting to know how to make the best decision. Especially with home furnishings, the investment can add up quickly and cost more than your car. So, is your car or your home more important to you and/or your spouse?

BRAND PROMISES AND THEIR EFFECT ON YOUR DECISIONS

Why do you select each item that you use each day? Is it because of function, beauty, brand, quality, convenience or all of the above?

How important are brands when making purchasing decisions? Each manufacturer has its own "brand promise" that provides shortcuts to select everything from shoes to home furnishings.

Even the selection of the color and type of car you drive tells others who you are and what is important to you. For example, Volvo's brand promise is safety, so you are telling the outside world that you value safety when you drive one.

TRENDS, BRANDS AND THEIR INFLUENCE

Are you influenced or impacted by trends? You may not think so, but the effectiveness of brand merchandising does impact what is available to you, and from those selections, you choose for yourself. If you purchase online or off the rack, your choices are limited to what the stores and merchandisers offer each season.

You shop at particular stores and stay at certain brands of hotels because they deliver a dependable and desirable experience.

Nordstrom is known for its customer service and the piano music that wafts through the store. When you shop at Nordstrom you have more than a visual experience; your auditory senses are entertained, whether you prefer the style of music or not. Nordstrom is different and memorable because of it. If any other department store added a grand piano, you would consider them a copycat. It is unique to Nordstrom's brand experience.

A W Hotel® delivers a different visual experience than a Days Inn®. You can get a good night's sleep at either hotel, or can you? This again is case of function versus form.

Tere Bresin, ASID, CID/Marisa Pellegrini, Photographer

WHERE TO GET DESIGN IDEAS

The Internet, social media and HGTV expand our access to design resources and knowledge. Who doesn't love to see the latest fashion and color trends? We like to be informed, whether we're fashion divas or not.

Fashion design and color trends used to precede home fashion by years, and now the two occur almost simultaneously. The Color Marketing Group predicts color trends as much as three years in advance, and that affects what choices you have now. Just look at a few fashion and shelter magazines side by side and you will see the similarities.

If you are driven by trends, you will need to replenish your budget more frequently. It may make sense to decide about your personal style and ignore the trends, unless you select a few accessories to update your space every few years.

When you have access to anything you can imagine or want, it actually makes your decisions more challenging. How do you choose? Start with why you are making each decision.

Exercise #2

Whether you're planning to do your project with professional guidance or not, it is a big task. The more you prepare yourself and discuss your priorities with your spouse or partner, the better. What you don't want to do is end up in a conflict over the design or financial decisions that accompany it, and answering these questions now will prevent problems later.

An interior designer will ask you most, if not all, of these questions so they understand your needs, desires, priorities and dreams.

- Why are you doing the project?
- Why is this important now?
- What will having a redesigned space do for you?
- How will it impact your life, family, efficiency, productivity, enjoyment, etc.?
- Do you have a deadline for the project (wedding, graduation, baby, etc.)?
- What would a successful project look like?
- Who is going to use the space?
- What is your scope of work? (Put everything on your wish list; you can edit it later.)
- How long are you planning to live in your home?
- What changes would you most like to have happen and why?
- How much are you willing to invest to accomplish those changes?
- How will you pay for the project?
- What do you like about your space now?
- What do you want to keep?
- What is your style?
- What are your biggest concerns about doing this project?
- Do you want to do the project yourself?
- Do you have time to manage your own project?
- If not, do you want to hire someone to assist you?
- Do you like or intend to shop?
- Do you value service and expertise and are you willing to invest in assistance?
- What are your goals in hiring someone to assist you?

- What are your concerns about hiring someone to help you?
- What do you value most: function, beauty, brand, quality, budget, trends, your time, convenience, or all of the above?
- Do you and your spouse or significant other agree on these values?
- If not, how will you resolve your differences?
- Who else will you ask for their opinions? Your kids, friends or other family members?
- Where do you spend the majority of your time, and how do you feel about those spaces?
- How do you want your guests and family to feel in your home?
- Why is that important to you?
- What do you want your home to say about your style, personality and priorities?
- Happy
- Joyful
- Serene
- Calm
- Easy-going
- Quiet
- Nurturing
- Cozy
- Inviting
- Cheerful
- Colorful
- Family-oriented
- Loving
- Sleek
- Sophisticated
- Exciting
- Energetic
- Exciting
- Funky
- Unique
- Environmentally conscious
- Pet-friendly
- Kid-friendly
- Designed for a home chef
- Spa-like
- Luxurious

- Refined
- Elegant
- Low-key (not ostentatious)
- Decorative
- Casual
- Formal
- Playful
- Quirky
- Impressive
- Relaxed
- Low maintenance
- Practical

Once you complete these questions, share your answers with each other if you are married or cohabitating, and resolve any disagreements between each of you before you spend a penny. You may be surprised at some of your partner's answers.

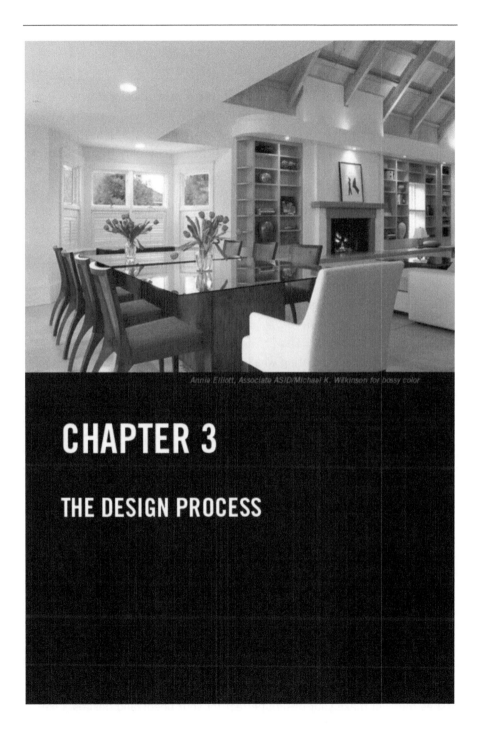

Annie Elliott, Associate ASID/Michael K. Wilkinson for bossy color

CHAPTER 3

THE DESIGN PROCESS

WHERE TO SHOP

If you are only interested in function and the lowest price, perhaps you will be happy shopping at a big box store like IKEA® where the prices are low due to the buying power of the chain. Many big box stores have a design staff that doesn't charge for their services, but they only design with the products they offer.

That may be okay for you, or perhaps a part of your project can be done with these stores so your home doesn't look like other IKEA® shoppers' homes.

If you want your home to look unique instead of "store bought," it takes more research, knowledge and resources. If a unique look is important to you, you have two options:

- Spend time evaluating what you like and don't like, shop for hours, weeks and months, get educated on how to design for yourself.
- Hire a professional to assist you.

It may be helpful to know the process an interior designer uses to help you achieve your vision because it is complex. It takes years of education and experience to develop design skills and knowledge, because it is more than just selecting pretty things. The options are limitless, and knowing how to edit and design well comes from practice.

DESIGN PROCESS: PROGRAMMING

After we discuss how we work and agree to move forward with a retainer and Letter of Agreement (aka Contract), we start the design process.

We mentioned the first step, Programming, in the last chapter. It is often easier for someone other than you and your partner to uncover all of the issues that will make your design perfect for your needs and desires. Like the architect and his wife, sometimes it helps to have a third party to extract and decipher the unsaid concerns so that you achieve the desired result.

Designers go beyond the interior to consider the orientation of your home on the property and the natural light that enters your space.

We look at the flow and use of your spaces, and we can quickly brainstorm ideas to expand the function and use of your space with creative layouts.

For example, we reviewed a pop-top (adding a floor) project and addition designed by an architectural firm and noticed that the kitchen was on the west side of the space when it could easily be on the east side so the client could enjoy the morning sun (which was one of their stated priorities). The redesign was minimal and created a tremendous improvement in the natural light during an important part of the day.

Understanding how to maximize the function of your space by changing lighting, plumbing, wall configurations, HVAC and materials to accomplish a different and more flexible use of the space is part of our expertise. We can guide you on the overall costs to accomplish your objectives within budget and on time with the help of our team of contractors, subcontractors and vendors.

One of our clients did not have a powder room in her 1930s home, and because she entertained frequently, she wanted one. We borrowed space from an oversized bathroom and added it to a hall closet to create one for her.

We changed the entry into the guest bedroom and closed a hall entry to the rescaled bathroom to make it an en suite space instead of a dual powder and guest bathroom. We added a linen cabinet to the en suite bathroom, so the function was actually improved without feeling cramped. What my client loved was the additional privacy and convenience for her overnight and daytime guests as well as the added functionality.

DESIGN PROCESS: CONCEPTUAL DESIGN AND SCHEMATICS

This is a magical part of the process. When we go back to our studio, we think, sketch, draw and redraw the first concepts for your space (space planning). We research the options, talk to our vendors and create a palette for your space, and we review codes if applicable.

Sometimes we bring in our contractor and subcontractors to find out if we can do what we envisioned, and to provide initial estimates. If we are using our vetted team, we tell them to hold time in the schedule for the estimated length of the project. If a project goes out to bid, you may not be able start and end the project as quickly, and if we haven't worked with the team, nor have you, we could experience challenges with the team dynamics, so it is important to ensure there is a good fit with the teams you hire.

You can also lose the valuable benefit of a long-term relationship that ensures that problems are solved quickly and easily—sometimes without you knowing they even existed. It's not to say that it can't work to put a project out to bid, but there are many considerations when selecting your team, and the lowest price at the beginning doesn't always ensure that the price is all-inclusive.

Once we know we can accomplish the design, we come back to you with our preliminary suggestions, materials, finishes, budgets and concepts for your input and approval.

Depending on the complexity of the project, this phase could include multiple meetings.

DESIGN PROCESS: DESIGN DEVELOPMENT

At this point, we are designing the details of the project. We draw elevations (vertical wall details), detailed drawings of specific design elements like cabinetry, and finalize floor plans.

If we are drawing your space for a renovation or addition, we create a full set of drawings, and if it requires an architect or engineer to stamp the drawing because of moving structural or load-bearing walls, we ensure this step is complete.

Drawings may include

- As-built drawings
- Floor plans
- Furniture plans
- Reflected ceiling plans (fixture locations and details)
- Electrical plans
- Elevations
- Sections
- Millwork (built-in cabinetry and trim—the millwork shop will also create shop drawings)
- Kitchens cabinet layouts
- Tile layouts
- Window treatments
- And more depending on the scope of your project

We finalize selections for all of your materials and finishes, write specifications and finalize details like the placement of towel rods and toilet paper holders for your bathrooms and the location of cabinet pulls.

We meet with the contractor and subcontractors during this phase to review the drawings and to ensure we answer their questions or concerns before they complete their pricing.

If we are managing the purchasing process for your project, we request and confirm final pricing from all of the vendors and create proposals for the furnishings, window treatments and other items we are coordinating on your behalf.

One piece of custom furniture could take hours to order. When you are specifying pattern matches, placement of multiple materials and trims—plus we request CFAs ("Cuttings from the actual bolts" aka Cuttings For Approval) to ensure they match the original samples—and start logging the details about the lead times, order details, etc., it can take more time than you might imagine.

Assuming the revised budget, drawings, selections and proposals meet with your approval, we proceed to the next step.

DESIGN PROCESS: CONTRACT DOCUMENTS AND SPECIFICATIONS

If the scope of work includes construction, we review the bids to ensure the bidders read the scope of work and details completely. In some cases, we may act as your agent to oversee the process and assist with scheduling. This is another time-consuming part of this phase and often requires detailed knowledge about construction, as well as blueprint and specification reading.

We help you decide who to hire and assist in moving the project forward. Some designers manage and coordinate the entire project management process.

If it is included in your scope of work, we execute purchasing on your behalf once you approve the orders and provide payment for the products. We follow up with the vendors; review acknowledgments to make sure everything is correct; process the paperwork; submit payments; coordinate shipments, delivery and installation of all items; and monitor to make sure everything is on schedule. If not, we inform you throughout the process.
We inspect the goods before delivery and resolve any problems on your behalf.

We have had shipments come in damaged even though the furniture was carefully wrapped. Some pieces actually leave the factory with damage under the wrapping, so quality control is not what it used to be. It is more common now than ever, and it is one of the most frustrating parts of our job to deal with the vendors and shippers.

INSTALLATION

After the items are inspected at the receiver's warehouse and the delivery and installation of the goods is arranged, we meet the movers to ensure that the orders are not damaged in transit from the receiver's warehouse. It happens. If so, we resolve those problems.

HGTV reality TV fans know that the "big reveal" days are emotional and exciting for clients. If you do your own project, you miss the huge impact of "Wow, this takes my breath away." It takes thousands of details that we micromanage on your behalf to create that big transformation. The pain of the process is always worth it, and either you can be responsible for it, or we can.

It's like having children, it takes months to create that miracle, and it is an amazing and emotional moment when you see your baby for the first time.

JOB FINALIZATION

We create or help you create a punch list of repairs and deficiencies, and make sure that everything is completed to our specifications and your satisfaction.

At this point, we add the icing to the cake with accessories and art if that is included in the scope of work.

As you can tell, any project takes a lot of time between the first meeting and the installation of the last item. Having a realistic expectation of time and fees and an appreciation for the value of not having to manage this yourself is important. Ask your designer and be open with him or her about your expectations and desired level of service so they stay within your preferred scope and budget.

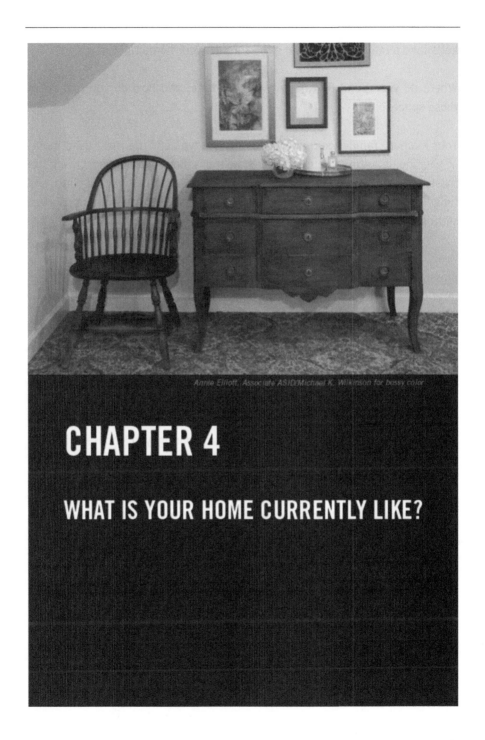

Annie Elliott, Associate ASID/Michael K. Wilkinson for bossy color

CHAPTER 4

WHAT IS YOUR HOME CURRENTLY LIKE?

Let's take a mental or physical stroll through your home right now.

Where do you spend the majority of your time, and how do you feel about those spaces?

Your kitchen, family room and bedrooms are typically the most used rooms of your home. When you consider how many hours you spend "living" in those spaces, doesn't it make sense to invest in quality furnishings and finishes that are durable, easy to maintain and that provide the perfect setting for the scrapbook of your life?

Your master suite is your respite from the chaos and overwhelming pressures of your day and the essential decisions such as the bed you sleep in and the mattress you sleep on can affect your health. Are you happy with your master suite? What would you like to change or enhance?

YOUR BATHROOM'S SAFETY AND FUNCTION ARE AS IMPORTANT AS ITS BEAUTY

Your bathroom's safety is affected by the flooring you choose and your shower's valve construction. The best selections prevent slips, falls and scalding.

As designers, we first consider your safety and your bathroom's function before considering the aesthetics of your space. We think of your plumbing fixtures as the jewelry of your bathroom.

The reason we redesigned our architect friend's master suite was because his neo-angle shower took up valuable floor space in the small bathroom and didn't provide much room for showering. By rearranging the fixtures and enclosing the toilet room next to the shower, and by adding privacy glass between the two spaces and on the doors, we added natural light to visually expand the feel of the spaces.

We installed more lighting on dimmers, a whirlpool tub, and a beautiful dual cabinet to complete the space. We added shelves in the master bedroom and crown molding in the coffers. We selected soothing colors and designed luxurious draperies to frame the windows.

Is your bathroom safe, is it functional, and does it visually please you? If not, what would you like to change?

Your bedroom's colors can evoke a subliminal emotional response and set the tone for your entire day, and they also create an environment for relaxation and love. Color evokes an emotional response, so it must be carefully considered because it contributes to the ambiance of each room.

A favorite design professor said, "The master bedroom is the boudoir, where the woman looks and feels sexy and relaxed, and the husband is the invited guest."

Now, mentally walk into your closet and visualize its organization and your wardrobe choices. Are the rods full of selections designed by well-known clothing brands, or are the majority of your clothes and shoes functional rather than stylish?

Is your closet constructed with builder-basic materials like expandable rods and shelves, or is it filled with a closet system including a well-designed layout for your lovelies? Having an organized closet with great lighting makes it easy to select your apparel for the day, and it starts your day with confidence. How would you like to change your closet's function or aesthetics?

Think about these questions for all areas of your home. If you work with an interior designer, you will be asked many questions just like these, and from your answers, your designer will create a design concept that aligns with your vision.

Exercise #3

What is your personal style?

- ☐ Modern/contemporary
- ☐ Traditional
- ☐ Transitional
- ☐ Minimal
- ☐ Tuscan
- ☐ Asian
- ☐ Southwestern
- ☐ Old world
- ☐ Mid-century modern
- ☐ Country
- ☐ Arts & crafts
- ☐ Cottage
- ☐ Beach/tropical
- ☐ Eclectic
- ☐ Other
- ☐ What colors or materials do you love and want to include in your home?
- ☐ What colors or materials do you dislike?

You and your partner should answer these questions, even if he or she says it doesn't matter. It matters when it affects your finances and your partner's comfort level with spending. You don't want to wait to find out how strongly the other person feels after the selections and investments have been made.

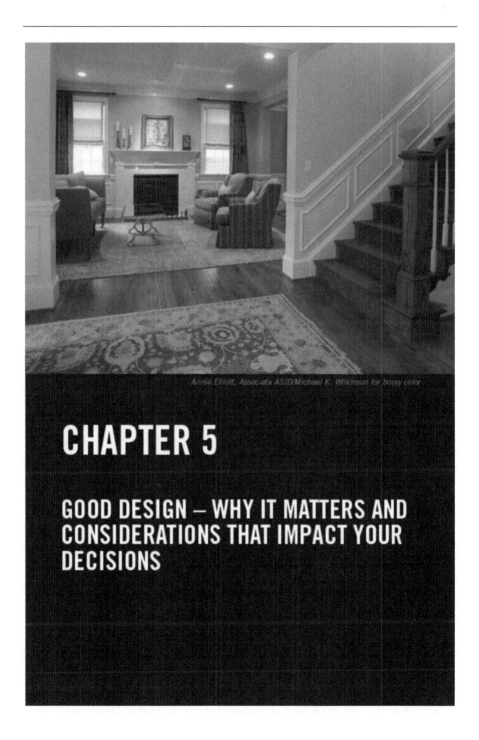

Annie Elliott, Associate ASID/Michael K. Wilkinson for bossy color

CHAPTER 5

GOOD DESIGN – WHY IT MATTERS AND CONSIDERATIONS THAT IMPACT YOUR DECISIONS

Sybil Barrido, ASID/Henry Cabala, Photographer

We mentioned "practical" design in the Preface, and what we mean by that is how well does your space function and how well is it organized? Is your home designed with durable materials that are easy to maintain? Is the investment for the design solution proportional to the results you want to achieve and can afford?

"Aesthetic design" is about the visual preferences like color and texture. Luckily, it is possible to have practical design that is also beautiful.

GOOD DESIGN: THE KITCHEN

Kitchens that are well-designed provide effortless access to the right tools located in the right place at the right time. If you take a hot dish out of the oven, the mitts need to be close to it. When you prepare vegetables, your knives and cutting board should be close to the prep sink.

If you are a gourmet cook that entertains friends and family regularly, commercial-grade appliances can make a noticeable difference in the quality of your food. Appliances are both an aesthetic and functional design decision.

Multiple refrigerator drawers positioned for access by more than one cook place fruits and vegetables next to a prep sink, or outside of the work zone for kids so they can access juices and drinks.

Dual dishwashers are a great feature for larger families and for entertaining households.

Storage of dishes, utensils, pots and pans can be made more functional by choosing drawers over cabinets with doors.

Good ventilation over your cooktop or range removes odors quickly and preserves the indoor air quality and furnishings within your home.

GOOD DESIGN: BATHROOMS

We spend a lot of time in our bathrooms, so the function, safety and aesthetics of these spaces are important.

Storage for supplies, makeup, shaving accoutrements, cleaning products, medications, first aid supplies and many more necessities can be optimized for accessibility and organization. Drawers are more functional than cabinets, but they are also more expensive. An alternative is to add storage bins to the cabinets if you want a less expensive option.

Vanity heights used to be 29- to 30-inches for bathrooms. Today, it is not unusual to have 36-inch high countertops or even multiple heights for different height users or if you have under-mount sinks. The lower heights can be made more functional for taller users by selecting vessel sinks.

Appropriate ventilation in your bathrooms controls odor and moisture and prevents mold and damage to your cabinets, windows and grout.

Shelley Gorman, Allied ASID/Eric Penrod, Photographer

Builder-basic lighting means that lighting for makeup or shaving is rarely considered. Simple changes like adding sconces at face-level or adding a lighted make-up mirror can improve your satisfaction with the function of your bathroom.

- Do you stand to apply your makeup and can you get close enough to the mirror that you can see what you are doing? Do you prefer to sit instead?
- Do you like clean countertops, or is it okaywith you to keep your hairdryer, toothbrush and other sundries on display?

- Do you have enough rods and hooks for towels, washcloths and hand towels to dry?
- Is there adequate storage for linens?

Stephen Pararo, ASID/Photos courtesy of Pineapple House Interior Design

GOOD DESIGN: BEDROOMS

Bedrooms perform more functions than they should for a variety of reasons. Perhaps it has to do with insufficient space within the home or a desire for privacy and quiet.

Children's rooms often include a desk for studying, and that means that the line is blurred between rest, play, sleep and homework.

The master suite may also include a desk area, and that means that work, bills and other distractions can keep you from relaxation, intimate encounters and sleep. Having an openly multifunctional space will affect your sense of escape from the most stressful parts of life. If you can move the desk areas to other spaces in the home, that is the optimal solution. If you can't, then consider desk systems that can close the paperwork from view, or use a screen or drapery to divide the space.

A good night's sleep also means that you need light control. If you require total darkness, then you can use black-out shades behind other window treatments that add a decorative flair to the room. Alternatively, you can use shutters or wood blinds, although the slats create light gaps.

The need for darkness to sleep is very different for each person, so ask your family members if they are having difficulty sleeping a full seven to eight hours a night.
As we age, temperature control becomes more important, too. Although many designers discourage the use of ceiling fans, they do provide air movement that makes the room more comfortable without additional cooling costs. Even in the winter, many people like the extra air flow.

Ultimately, you need to sleep because it is necessary for good health, so function wins in this case.

And, a great mattress is essential. Manmade materials can "off-gas" and smell bad for months, so if that is a concern, then research natural product lines that don't include chemicals. Replace your mattress every 10 years if you can because the support and the cleanliness of the mattress declines and impacts your health. Replace your pillows every six months to a year, and use washable covers under your pillow cases.

Stephen Pararo, ASID/Photos courtesy of Pineapple House Interior Design

GOOD DESIGN: FAMILY AND GREAT ROOMS

A common frustration for interior designers is the placement of televisions and audio equipment. We don't like to display the TV openly because of our aesthetic preferences, but today, the newer technology makes it less offensive. We know we won't win the battle with all families, so at least consider enclosing or encasing your TV in an attractive cabinet.

If your space is multifunctional, meaning that it is open to your kitchen and you like to watch cooking shows when you prepare your family's meals, then having a TV within viewing distance makes a lot of sense.

A splurge would be electronic lifts to hide the TV below a countertop or in a cabinet.

Since the seating in this area gets lots of use, invest in high-quality, cleanable materials. If the fabric you use is lighter colored, fabric protection can be added later.

Multifunctional furniture solves many design challenges today. An example would be a coffee table with an optional cushion that turns it into an ottoman. You can also find coffee tables with ottomans or bins underneath that add flexible seating and storage for unsightly remotes.

Don't forget blackout shades if you want to achieve a home theater experience.

A high-end option is motorization and multiple layers for your window treatments. This is especially useful for large or tall windows or a large number of windows in a room.

ADDITIONAL "GOOD DESIGN" CONSIDERATIONS

The concept of good design includes more complex factors today than ever. With aging parents that want to stay home rather than go into an assisted living facility, or environmental sensitivities and allergies, it takes more knowledge and research to accommodate these needs. How a senior's home is designed means the difference between independence for more years or dependence on family members and health care providers.

GOOD DESIGN: LIGHTING AND TECHNOLOGY

Spaces are more functional when they are lit properly. Some areas just need ambient lighting and others require task lighting for reading, cooking or makeup. The bulbs or "lamps" that are used within the fixtures affect how colors appear, so these are important design decisions. If, perhaps, traditional incandescent lighting isn't available, your home interior will look different because you must choose different lamping for your fixtures.

Paint or fabric colors may look fabulous in the store and completely different in your home during the day, dusk or night time. Ambient lighting from your light fixtures can also contribute to color shifts.

Unfortunately, many homes do not have adequate lighting, and it impacts the beauty and functionality of the spaces.

More light is necessary to see when you age, and your perception of color changes as well. If you are an art collector, then lighting becomes vitally important when displaying your treasures. A lighting designer specializes in creating the right balance to enhance your collection.

The ultimate in lighting and automation design includes remote control panels, lighting of scenes such as parties, audio/visual and communications technology. If you have 20-foot ceilings and want to have functional window treatments, motorization may be required.

Your current switches can be retrofitted with Radio RA® switches so you can dim multiple fixtures with a remote. If you are building a new home, you can also pre-wire your space with special multifunctional switching systems.

Electronic needs are met with wireless routers, which provide much more flexibility with the placement of computers, printers and smart TVs; however, you may need repeaters so the signals are picked up in remote areas of your home.

Most homes don't have a home theater, but you can achieve near-theater conditions with careful planning.

Don't forget to think about noise control if the TV or theater area is adjacent to bedrooms.

Jennifer Markanich, Allied ASID/Steven Long, Photographer

GOOD DESIGN: HEALTH AND SAFETY

Interior design affects the usability of our spaces. If you need to accommodate an aging parent with physical or visual challenges in your home, or a person with special needs, then your interiors may need to be remodeled. A simple decision like adding grab bars to the bathroom requires extra blocking (between the studs) to support the weight of the user.

If you have a family member with limited mobility, flooring material choices affect their ability to move safely and with ease. Visual cues for floor elevation and material changes are also important. Contrast of flooring colors can help the aging eye discern the differences and can prevent missteps or tripping.

Bathrooms are the most dangerous areas of the home, even for healthy people. Hazards like slippery floors can result in falls and severe injuries.

Seemingly simple decisions about materials and finishes are critically important in all areas of your home when designing for the elderly or others using assistive devices. Select slip-resistant tile or stone when choosing materials and avoid area rugs that could cause a trip or fall.

A neighbor's daughter and her husband decided that it was time to move home to take care of her aging father. We designed an addition and reworked a main floor bathroom so her father could live on the main floor and use the accessible bathroom without the risk of slipping and falling. We rebuilt the shower so it did not have a curb and added a seat and grab bars to the shower and to the toilet area. Their budget was tight, so we used simple white wall tile and a non-slip ceramic floor tile.

The result eased my client's worry about her father's safety when he used the bathroom alone, and he was able to maintain his independence and pride longer as a result of this transformation.

Stephen Pararo, ASID/Photos courtesy of Pineapple House Interior Design

GOOD DESIGN: AIR QUALITY

Indoor air quality is affected by the materials and finishes of an interior. Formaldehyde, glues, dyes, preservatives, coatings, finishes, paint components and cushioning are a few of the contributors to toxic fumes your family or coworkers may be exposed to on a daily basis. If a family member is chemically sensitive or asthmatic, the material and finish choices you make are critical to their health.

If you have babies or young children in your home, it is important to consider the materials that surround them during their formative years because it can affect their long-term health.

Just like children's pajamas, fabrics must meet certain standards for flammability. Some commercial spaces require higher standards than others, and even in your home, the safety of U.S.-manufactured fabrics may be higher than imported products. An interior designer is trained to know about this design factor.

Lower cost options often use components with lower durability and more chemicals, so price becomes a factor when selecting interior products.

GOOD DESIGN: DURABILITY

Another issue is durability of materials and construction. Some materials are better suited for applications than others. Many fabrics are tested for durability, and that is especially important for high-use areas of your home. Using the right fabric for upholstery will ensure your investment lasts and looks better longer.

The long-term durability of your cabinets is affected by the type of construction as well as the components used. Cabinets may be constructed out of particle board, MDF (medium density fiberboard), plywood with a veneer, or hardwood. If they are constructed from particle board or MDF, they may not be strong enough to support a heavy slab of granite.

Dove-tailed joints are one of the best options for construction. Even drawer glides can affect the function and longevity of your investment.

GOOD DESIGN: ERGONOMICS

Ergonomics is the study of designing equipment and devices that fit the human body, its movements and its cognitive abilities.

Even in your home, ergonomics is important. If the men in the household are tall and large-boned and the women in the household are small and petite, one standard chair will not fit both sizes.

For one client couple, the wife was 5'1" and the husband was 6'2," so we had to custom design their kitchen chairs that worked for both of them.

Task chairs for desks, drawers for keyboards, locations of storage in the kitchen, or the installation of bathroom fixtures should consider the ergonomics of the users. Even countertop heights in kitchens and bathrooms should be established based on the users' comfort.

GOOD DESIGN: CONSERVATION AND GREEN DESIGN

This topic is very complex and may not be a high priority for you, so our intent is to make you aware of sustainable or green design. Several great books are available on the topic, and we recommend doing your homework if this is important to you.

If you are concerned about the environment, select materials from sustainable forests or from recycled materials. Some consumers may think that "green" products are more expensive, but that is not necessarily the case.

Our homes emit more pollution into the air than we realize, and though you may own just one home and not feel that your contribution is of any concern, it really is. The global effect of pollution from each home added together impacts our planet's health and our children's futures.

Shelley Gorman, Allied ASID/Eric Penrod, Photographer

Annie Elliott, Associate ASID/Michael K. Wilkinson for bossy color

CHAPTER 6

PRIORITIZING YOUR INVESTMENT

Trade-offs happen every day with what you want versus what you set-aside financially for your project. Maybe you want granite countertops, but with the fabrication cost, the slabs you like may exceed what you want to or can spend.

You do have options, and that's why a budget must be developed before selecting materials. "Value-engineering" your project is a must if you don't want to give up your granite.

- You can always install granite tile countertops or select slab granite for your island and use another material elsewhere.
- Or, you can select a less expensive cabinet without the specialty finish to cut expenses.
- Or, you can still invest in your favorite cabinets and select a different countertop that you can replace in the future.

The higher the quality and durability of a product, the higher the price, typically. Counterintuitively, a higher price for a product does not necessarily guarantee durability and quality. Some costs are higher because of a brand's perceived value.

Manufacturers spend millions of dollars building brand awareness, and that comes with a price. When you select based on brand, you select what you believe that brand promises. Consumers often select brands as a shortcut. Selecting a brand isn't the only option though. Value depends on your perception. If you are not sure of the quality or value of an item, seek professional guidance.

Investing in the best materials for the application doesn't mean you must break your budget. If you use your family room every single day for hours a day, then you may want to invest in the best quality sofa and fabric that you can manage. It will last longer and look better during its life. We call that the product lifecycle.

Your sofa can be slip-covered or re-upholstered, and that can often cost as much as a new sofa. Leather may be a great option unless you have animals with claws that sleep on your furniture. The materials you choose must fit within your lifestyle and budget criteria.

If you get tired of things easily, then you may want to invest in different pillows to change the look of a higher quality sofa that you intend to keep for a long period of time.

You can invest less in the other furnishings in the room to balance your budget.

Darla Blake, ASID/Dan Steinberg, Photographer

FINANCIAL DECISIONS AND THE ECONOMY

After the economic downturn of 2007 and 2008, many consumers pulled back from investing in non-essentials. And though spending is increasing, decisions about where to invest are noticeably different. Consumers are opting for value and function over ostentatious spending.

The real estate market's decline makes decisions more difficult when the financing for projects must come from savings instead of borrowing against diminished home equity. Now, making decisions about where the money is spent may mean choosing between private schools or a kitchen remodel, or a boat versus a bath remodel.

If you plan to live in your home for at least five to ten years, you may decide to invest more in the renovation because it improves your quality of life and enjoyment of your home; and it may result in postponing your decision to move because you love your home that much more.

If you plan to stay in your home less than five years, painting and redecorating may be a better and more economical option.

Renting over owning is a clear choice for many consumers today, and that means you don't have to worry about renovating. You can invest in furnishings you love.

DESIGN VS. DECORATING

Design and decorating are more popular than ever thanks to the "reality TV" shows. Although the words are often used interchangeably, design involves more than just selecting beautiful items; it includes function, form and utilization, while decorating is more about the aesthetic choices.

The Internet has made it easier to shop globally, and yes, you are fully qualified to shop, especially if you are a female. You may spend hours and days and weeks looking and looking for the perfect coffee table. It is an obsession for some of us. However, remember that lasting beauty involves more than the initial visual appearance of your home.

Maybe you love the process and the adventure of finding bargains. And maybe you can find better prices for individual items when you shop online. Be sure to compare "apples to apples" though. Often what looks like a similar sectional sofa for less money may be using a lower grade of cushioning, such as chemically infused foam, a lower grade of fabric, MDF construction and no springs.

The same look by a designer may be manufactured with a high-quality, durable fabric, hardwood construction and eight-way hand-tied springs with a down casing on the cushions. This "to-the-trade" product (one that sells only through design professionals) may be selected because the vendor is meticulous about matching patterns and consistently standing behind the product. The two sofas may look alike, but the construction could affect its long-term durability. Maybe you consider it a splurge to invest in quality construction, and if so, be sure to select the pieces used the most in your room for the extra dollars. If your budget won't allow you to invest in the better quality, consider waiting to purchase key pieces.

Because investing in your home and its furnishings depends on your financial means and your values toward such investment, many publications and even TV programs show you options to achieve the "designer look" on a budget.

Stephen Pararo, ASID/Photos courtesy of Pineapple House Interior Design

REMODELING AND CONSTRUCTION DESIGN

If you are remodeling or designing your home from the ground up, you will probably need some assistance to accomplish the results you desire, unless you are a 100 percent do-it-yourselfer that has spent a considerable amount of time researching, organizing and planning for your project.

You will likely hire a general contractor or builder, and perhaps an architect and an interior designer or interior decorator. If you are remodeling a bathroom or kitchen, you may want to hire a kitchen and bath specialist. Some interior designers are also specialists in both areas. A seasoned designer can design a remodel or construction project that maximizes your space and saves you money in the end. Specialists focus on one type of design and consistently research for new innovations and ideas.

Since you probably work full time at a job or raising your family, unless you are trained and work in the field, you will not have the breadth of knowledge that a professional has that does it every day. It takes lots of experience and practice to understand the intricacies of construction.

It is also important to understand factors such as how materials are installed, maintenance requirements, durability, how to select fabricators, the most reliable vendors and much more.

Yes, you can read books, watch "reality TV" and design your own spaces. You can even shop for materials, hire the subcontractors and contractor, and manage the project yourself. You are ultimately responsible for the result, and that can be exciting and scary at the same time.

On one project, the plumber called to discuss the location of the pump for the whirlpool tub. Our hearts sank when we noticed that the tub looked pinkish and not creamy. The contractor thought it was because the lighting was poor, but when he shone the work light on the tub, there was no doubt it was the wrong color.

When the plumber returned, we asked what color he ordered and he confirmed with his first purchase order he had ever used that Biscuit, the correct color, was ordered. We checked the crate, and Innocent Blush was the color stamped on the crate. If the plumber had installed the tub, he would have had to pay for a new one.

The project was delayed by eight weeks, and the client wasn't happy, but since they weren't living in the house during the renovation, they didn't have to suffer through the extended project. This error hurt the contractor because his schedule was destroyed and he had to pull off the project to wait for the replacement tub to arrive.

A good designer protects you from making mistakes that can far exceed their fees. Their experience in designing spaces comes from education and practice. Design is like riding a bicycle. You start with training wheels and your parent holds onto the handlebars until you are confident and experienced. The more you ride, the better you get. Great design skills come from years of practice and constant immersion in the details of a business that just happens to provide beautiful design results.

A designer's value is much greater than just their aesthetic skills. Because interior designers typically work with a team of contractors, subcontractors and vendors they've known for years, their well-oiled team is willing to work through the inevitable challenges on projects.

It saves you time and money and lots of heartache when things go wrong. A team that knows one another so well they can predict what the other person will say when facing a decision is invaluable. Will the team be the least expensive if you were to put the project out to bid? Not necessarily, but you know the old expression, "You get what you pay for."

When you hire a professional, you are making a decision to trust an expert to walk you through the entire process. The value is in avoiding risk and managing a complex process so you can focus on what is most important to you—your life, your family and friends, and your time. It's important to hire someone with a design aesthetic that appeals to you, and yet that is just a small part of what it takes to create a masterpiece.

What you really want is the result of the beautiful design. The reason you are investing is because you want a different lifestyle. Maybe you want to have the most beautiful home in your neighborhood as a source of pride and enjoyment. If you are tackling a large-scale project and have the time and resources to manage and learn as you go, that is entirely your choice.

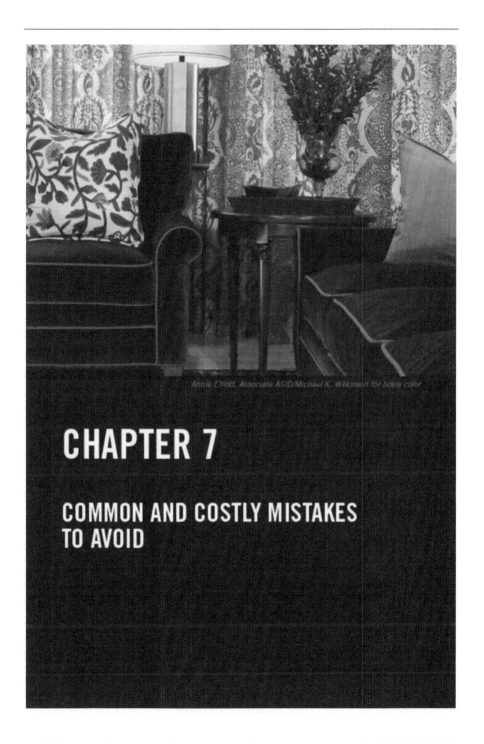

Annie Elliott, Associate ASID/Michael K. Wilkinson for bossy color

CHAPTER 7

COMMON AND COSTLY MISTAKES TO AVOID

There is no such thing as a trouble-free, easy breezy project. Fabrics get discontinued, shipments get lost or damaged, and subcontractors don't show up or have "personal issues." Even design professionals make mistakes, like transposing numbers on fabric orders. For instance, on one job, we ordered a Cutting For Approval (CFA) to check a cutting from the actual fabric bolt against the sample we selected. We received the CFA and it was green, and the actual selection was a deep rose.

It was accidental on our part, and if the fabric had shipped directly to the workroom without requesting a CFA, it could have cost our firm $25,000 to remake the draperies, and it would have added two months to the project. For many small design firms, a $25,000 mistake is more profit than they net at the end of the year, so it could bankrupt the designer.

Because design mistakes can be expensive, it is important to know the potential pitfalls that you could face if you do your own project. The following mistakes are common and preventable.

SCALE

Selecting the right-sized items for each space is a matter of balance, proportion and scale. A professional designer is trained to choose the right combination of selections to work harmoniously in your home. It is instinctive, but it is also practiced.

When the scale is wrong, you know it the minute you walk in a space. A sofa can be under-scaled for a large room and look as if it is made for a doll house. A sofa can also be over-scaled, and it can overwhelm the space. Either mistake can cost you thousands of dollars. Most consumers live with the mistake for years until it is time to replace the original mistake.

Before you purchase, be sure to create a scaled furniture plan to ensure each item will fit. Don't forget about your doorways, stairs and elevators before purchasing a large piece. Make sure you can get it into your house and the intended room. Tight hallways can make it challenging to bring in a long sofa.

A homeowner purchased his own furnishings, and when his two matching wedge sofas arrived, they wouldn't fit in the high-rise freight elevator, so he had to hire a crane to bring them in over the balcony. It was his problem to solve since he handled the ordering himself.

Stephen Pararo, ASID/Photos courtesy of Pineapple House Interior Design

PROPORTION

Proportion can relate to components of a piece, too. Perhaps you want comfortable club chairs for a family room. If the arms are bulbous like Popeye's forearm, the chairs may not look good if you have a coffee table with delicate legs nearby. The chairs may look great in the store and feel comfortable, but it is important to consider the type of space and each item that is in the room as well.

A chandelier may appear huge in the catalog, and when it is installed, it looks tiny and distant in a 20' high entryway.

Before hiring a designer, a homeowner purchased a costly French armoire for tens of thousands of dollars. It was out of scale for the room, so it ended up in the garage because the piece was too large and out of proportion for the space.

When proportion is exactly right, the result looks effortless. When it is wrong, the room looks unbalanced and individual items are "noticeable," and that means they are not right. Great design is understated, as if it has been that way forever.

If you are unsure of scale, use cardboard to create a model and test it in your space, or use blue tape on the floor to outline the size of the furniture.

Hint ... when a room comes together piece by piece, your tendency is to judge the individual pieces separately. It is best to suspend judgment until the whole space is complete. Allow yourself time to adjust to the changes. Sometimes it takes a few weeks to decide that you are completely in love. It's like dating. Love-at-first-sight is wonderful, yet it doesn't happen every time.

Stephen Pararo, ASID/Photos courtesy of Pineapple House Interior Design

DURABILITY

It is worth waiting to invest in durable, high-quality furnishings. Don't rush into a project unless you are willing to invest in the major seating pieces that your family will use every day. Make sure the decision makers have a chance to sit in a similar piece by the same manufacturer. It should be a unanimous decision. Even if your partner doesn't want to be involved, if it is used daily, it is a necessary sacrifice. The "tush" test is important.

If your partner really cares about having a comfortable chair, there are attractive and comfortable options that aren't noticeably recliners with the puffy fabric and a huge lever.

Durability is more than skin deep, so ask questions about the construction of the pieces. If you don't know about quality construction, ask a professional or shop in a quality store that will educate you about it. There is a reason one piece of furniture is significantly less expensive than another.

A client shopped online to find a less expensive option for two matching console tables and found the look she wanted. Unfortunately, the color was wrong for the space, and the doors were not properly cut and installed. The hinges were flimsy, yet she wanted the pieces. We customized them with a faux finish and hand embellishment. Re-fitting the doors was required, and in the end, the client spent more on these low quality pieces than if she had purchased high-quality pieces in the first place.

Fabrics available "to-the-trade" are woven with more complexity and quality than many options you see online. Some of these fabrics are constructed with finer fibers and dye processes than you can get at retail. It's not that every piece you select should use top quality designer fabrics, but when you invest in a few quality pieces, your room makes a more impactful design statement.

Invest in the best you can afford for your key pieces, especially those you use every day. Besides, you don't want to add to the landfill with products that deteriorate in a short period of time, do you?

APPROPRIATE FINISHES AND MATERIALS

Some low cost and imported products have fewer coats of finish than high quality hand-rubbed solid wood or high-quality veneers.

Veneered products' quality depends on the construction of the underlying substrate, and the mil thickness of the veneer. Veneered products may be an excellent option especially because varying climates can affect solid wood pieces and result in cracking of the components.

Few manufacturers talk about the finish's durability, so if you purchase low cost items, you may find the durability to be sub-par. Let the buyer beware.

BUYING ONLINE

When you see an item online, do you know for certain that it is exactly the same as something you see in a store or that your designer shows you? Many products are imported today, and though the look is similar, the quality may be different than you really want. If you choose a dining table online, what are your risks when you use a vendor that ships foreign products? You take on 100 percent of the liability and time to resolve the problems that come from ordering inferior, low-priced products that "look great" but won't stand up to normal wear and tear.

A client's housekeeper was cleaning the black "granite" vanity countertop that the builder purchased online. She called in a panic because the cleaning compound bleached the countertop. It turned out the cabinet was imported from China, and the "black" was created by mixing toner cartridge ink blended into a resin product. The solution? Replacement of the countertop.

What happens when you place an order and your new table or chairs arrive damaged? What if the wood splits because it was manufactured in a humid climate and your home is in an arid climate? That, unfortunately, is now your problem to resolve. If the wood splits because it wasn't manufactured for your climate, the manufacturer won't fix it, so you'll have to pay for a costly repair.

On a "fix-and-flip" (a house we purchased, remodeled in a few months and resold for a profit) project, we ordered an attractive-looking double cabinet with glass sinks from an e-Bay™ vendor. It was shipped directly to the job site. The box was destroyed en route, and the vanity was irreparably damaged. After contacting the vendor (who quickly closed his business), the freight company and e-Bay™, we realized we were out of luck. No refund was issued to us, and the loss was over $2,000. It took several weeks to find and receive a replacement.

BUDGET DILEMMAS

If you plan to furnish a room from scratch, what are you willing to spend? Do you know how much things cost at retail? If not, take some time to educate yourself about the costs of similar-looking options.

What is your comfort level for investing extra money in an individual piece and adjusting the overall project budget? It may make sense, and yet it may force you to make compromises that you don't like.

Where consumers get into trouble is not being prepared for what a project could cost. For example, if you have many great pieces that you want to use or perhaps refurbish, your budget could be as low as 10 percent of the value of your home. If you are starting from scratch and want to refurnish your entire home, your investment could be as much as 50 to 100 percent of the value of your home if you are investing in significant art or antiques.

If you are considering a major investment in your home, hiring a professional design consultant can save you money, stress and time. The designer's fees can be 10 to 30 percent of the overall budget for the project, and if you consider your time and the cost of mistakes, it may be well worth the investment because their discounts on "to-the-trade" goods can also save you money.

In the end, the designer's fees and advice may be a wash, and well worth the investment. It is up to you to decide what your comfort level is and your financial resources for this purpose.

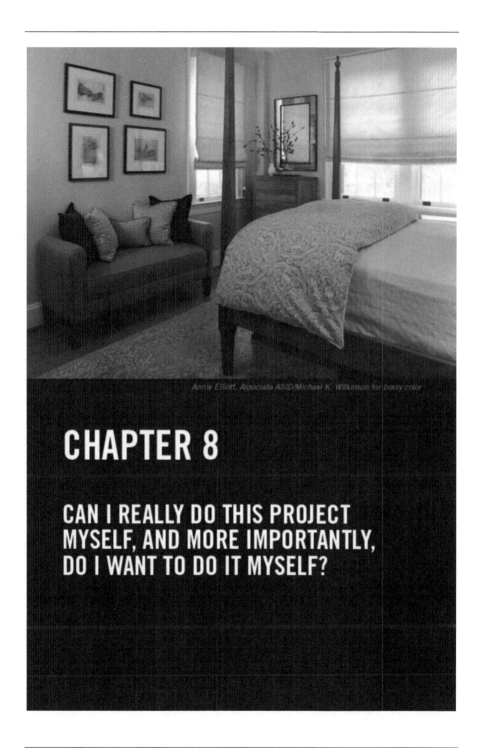

Annie Elliott, Associate ASID/Michael K. Wilkinson for bossy color

CHAPTER 8

CAN I REALLY DO THIS PROJECT MYSELF, AND MORE IMPORTANTLY, DO I WANT TO DO IT MYSELF?

Tere Bresin, ASID, CID/Marisa Pellegrini, Photographer

If you are planning to design your own space, you have complete control and responsibility for your results. If you have a great eye and receive compliments from your friends and family, the challenge can be fun and rewarding. It can also cost you a lot of money when problems occur.

Challenges occur even for professionals, and because they have long-term relationships with their vendors and tradespeople, they are often able to resolve problems on your behalf.

We ordered a Nepalese hand-tufted wool and silk rug for a client, and when it arrived it looked beautiful and she was thrilled. We received an angry call an hour later because, apparently, the rug was packed before it was dry, and it smelled terrible. The rug cost $15,000, and the client was understandably upset.

We called the showroom and they sent a rep to examine the rug and take it for cleaning. The rug went back and forth three times to the specialty cleaner, and the last time, it came back out of shape, shorter and narrower, and it looked worn. The showroom agreed to take it back, or we would have had to absorb the cost.

The client was so traumatized that she was unwilling to order a replacement and wait for another four months. We finally found a nice looking wool and silk rug at Restoration Hardware, so she spent less than $2,000 and was willing to accept a stock look in lieu of another potentially painful experience.

We were relieved that the showroom stood behind the product.

What if that had happened to you? What would you have done, and would the retailer or online resource stand behind the product? Be sure to check the stated policies.

What happens when something goes wrong or your merchandise gets damaged in transit? Do you have time to deal with that problem on top of your other responsibilities? It is great to save money, but when it costs you valuable time to fix problems it can extremely frustrating.

Once you answer the following questions, you may feel more certain than ever that you want to design your home yourself. Or, you may find that it is more than you want to manage yourself.

- Do you enjoy shopping? If you get overwhelmed with the choices and don't enjoy the process, you may want to hire help.
- Do you have time to shop? This goes back to the decision about the value of your free time. You might have time, but do you want to sacrifice it to "save money?"
- Do you have time to do research both online and offline through books and magazines? It can be fun, but will the items you select work well together? What if they don't and you've spent thousands of dollars and it doesn't look right? We've been hired to fix a client's mistakes on many occasions.
- If you don't have the natural talent, or you find it challenging, scary or financially risky to do your own work, you should probably hire a professional.

- Do you have contacts and resources that are reliable and dependable—specifically contractors and subcontractors if you are doing a remodeling or new construction project? If you haven't worked with the trades before, do you feel confident that you can problem-solve design issues and be available during the day in case of emergency?
- Do you know how to create and manage a complex project schedule and to ensure that everything arrives on time so the contractor and subcontractors are able to complete their work on time? If not, you need help.
- Did you know if you purchase products yourself that you are responsible for ensuring that all of the parts are in the boxes? If not, your subcontractors may charge extra for time and materials, and it can delay your job if they have to find parts.

Never do a construction project without a building permit, because it protects you from substandard work. If you sell your home in the future, your Realtor will ask for verification that all work was permitted. If a building inspector drives by and sees evidence of work being done without a permit or a neighbor turns you in, you can be forced to stop work, pay fines and even start the project from scratch. It's not worth the risk of working without a permit.

If these questions and answers don't worry you, then perhaps you are ready to do your project on your own. Start small so you don't take on more than you are ready to do. You will build confidence with small successes. If these answers do worry you, then you may want to hire a professional to assist you.

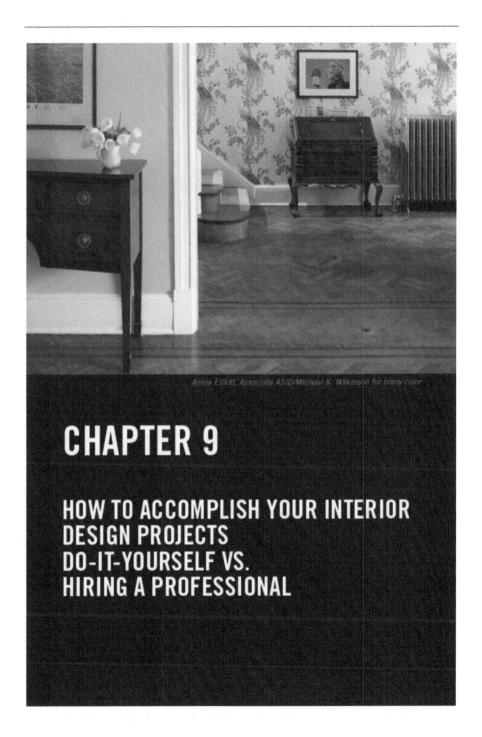

Annie Elliott, Associate ASID/Michael K. Wilkinson for bossy color

CHAPTER 9

HOW TO ACCOMPLISH YOUR INTERIOR DESIGN PROJECTS DO-IT-YOURSELF VS. HIRING A PROFESSIONAL

Crawford Z. Barnes, Allied ASID and Eileen Meilunas/Mark Worden, Photographer

DO-IT-YOURSELF

If you are ready to spend time getting educated about design, and you are ready to tackle it no matter what, then you should do it. You can always get help later if you get stuck.

Go to **http://www.HowToDesignYourPerfectInterior.com** to get our free *How To Design Your Perfect Interior Workbook* to organize your project. Just provide your name and email and you will receive the downloadable forms to insert in your own 4-inch binder.

We will walk you through the process in the next chapter.

DESIGN ADVICE PLUS DO-IT-YOURSELF

Some designers will create a design concept and master plan for you. The prices may be a few hundred dollars for a single room to thousands of dollars depending on the size and scope of your project and the skill and reputation of the designer. A design professional's expertise and resources can save you hundreds of hours of your time and prevent many costly and embarrassing mistakes.

The resources that designers use are beyond what is available to consumers.

It takes years to find the resources and learn exactly how to design and execute custom furnishings. If you are interested in purchasing on your own and yet want a few special pieces, discuss it with a designer.

ONLINE DESIGNERS

Designers that offer online services typically sell packages such as furniture plans, product and finish selections and paint selections.

Some offer consultation online so you can get direct feedback about your project and selections. They may use a service like Skype™ or Go To Meeting to review your project with you. What they deliver to you could be a furniture plan, sketches, paint colors, list of recommended products and/or commentary about how to execute the plan.

These same designers may also offer ongoing consultation and advice. Each website offer and designer is different.

Some designers do not offer online services because they prefer full-service projects, or they haven't considered doing it, and may not have the processes and technology in place to provide services in this way. It never hurts to ask if this is the level of service you are considering.

This is your least expensive paid option for hiring a professional interior designer and can save you weeks of time and thousands of dollars in mistakes if you purchase the wrong scale or size, wrong paint color for your space, and many other "faux pas" that can occur when doing it yourself.

Shelley Gorman, Allied ASID/Eric Penrod, Photographer

FULL-SERVICE INTERIOR DESIGN FIRMS

Most interior designers have completed formal education specific to the field. Designers learn the following skills through education and experience:

Space planning and utilization – This includes how the walls and furniture lay out for best function, productivity, ergonomics and aesthetics.

- Furniture planning – Designers can plan for the best function and aesthetics.
- Drawing – These skills can range from sketching to full-scale architectural drawings, computer-aided design (CAD), hand and computer rendering, so you can visualize exactly what your spaces will look like.
- Materials and finishes – Designers possess expertise in durability, use, maintenance and selection criteria for different applications.
- Textiles – This includes knowledge of construction and dye processes, durability and selection criteria for different applications.
- Building codes – Especially in commercial projects, designers must know applicable codes to meet minimum construction standards so projects pass inspection and are safe for the occupants.
- Color psychology, theory, formulation and consultation – Understanding color theory, component hues, shades, tints and combinations results in the best selections—certain colors when combined do not look good together because they cause color shifts when adjacent to one another. This is one of the many skills designers learn.
- Shopping – Most designers offer shopping services. If you have a limited budget, designers can review your selections or even shop online or at retail with you. Designers also shop for their full-service projects using "to-the-trade" resources that work specifically with designers and architects that understand the process of specifying custom furnishings. Shopping can be a big area of conflict because the designer is managing a whole project and selecting the best resources at the best value that is available using dependable resources. This is even more important today because many vendors are financially unstable after the last few years of the recession. Sometimes you will find something for less money online, and if you prefer to shop for yourself, please be

direct with the designer up front. Or, if midway into the project you want to look online or at retail, let the designer know immediately. Yes, you'll probably find items for less money, and yet there are valid reasons a designer uses a local vendor they've worked with for years.

It is because they know the vendor produces great quality and stands behind the products they sell. Just remember, not all items online are the equivalent to designer-resourced products. If the designer's choices are outside of your financial comfort zone, then say so.

Stephen Pararo, ASID/Photos courtesy of Pineapple House Interior Design

- Budgeting – A good designer understands that you have a budget.

  Even the wealthiest clients with "unlimited budgets" don't want to spend frivolously or unnecessarily. If you don't share what you expect to invest, it can lead to a "divorce" from your designer. If you have no idea what a reasonable budget is for the work you want to have done, then it is worth investing in advice from a designer that will listen to what you want to achieve and that will help you develop a plan to accomplish your desired outcome. If you don't talk openly, you can overspend what you had in mind and then you will be unhappy. Even if you learned not to talk about money growing up, remember that if you work with a designer, they should take the role as a trusted advisor. Designers can help you "value engineer" (meaning find ways to cut costs without sacrificing the design intent) to fit as much of your wish list as possible into your budget.

- Construction detailing – This includes selecting and designing materials and finishes including designing millwork (built-in cabinetry and trim). Some designers specialize in construction and remodeling design, and this can be immensely helpful to you when, for example, your builder or remodeler will seemingly ask you at the last minute to make a major decision when you are the busiest. Forcing you to make a critical decision under pressure can add to your stress level and delay your project and cost you more money. A designer that specializes in construction can guide you to make the right decisions quickly and easily and keep the builder on schedule and under budget. Construction requires hundreds of decisions, and an expert can make this easy for you.
- Aging in place and special needs design – If a family member has physical challenges, a space or even the entire home can be redesigned and remodeled to allow them to be independent. This is a specialty, so you want to ask questions to see if a designer has specific expertise and training in this area.
- Sustainable design – Some designers have extensive knowledge and even LEED certification, which means they completed additional training in products, materials and construction with "green" products.
- Historic design and restoration – If you're redesigning an historic home or building, some designers specialize in this type of work and understand what products can and can't be used to maintain the historic designation and integrity of the project.

Stephen Pararo, ASID/Photos courtesy of Pineapple House Interior Design

- Kitchen and bath design – This is another technical area that requires a great deal of knowledge about construction—plumbing, electrical, storage, etc. Bathrooms and kitchens are the most renovated and used areas of the home. If you want to upgrade to commercial appliances and customized cabinet interiors, steam showers, vessel tubs, custom cabinets for specific uses, built-in accessories like knife blocks, pop-up mixer stands, recycling centers, and hundreds of other features that make your space functional and beautiful, it is worth consulting with a specialist. Understanding how these items are installed requires extremely specific knowledge and experience. Even tile design is a specialty that some designers love because it creates a big impact on these spaces. You can hire a certified kitchen and bath designer, and in some cases, interior designers are certified and specialize in both general interior design and kitchen and bath design.

Glenn Gissler, ASID/Gross & Daley, Photographer

- Lighting design – This is an extremely technical area and a very small number of designers are specialists. Most designers are fairly knowledgeable about lighting, but if you have an important art collection, or you are particular about color, highlighting, mood and task lighting or electronic controls, you may wish to retain a specialist.

- Audio/visual and communication technology – This is also a highly technical area of design, and a limited number of designers are knowledgeable about this. If you want to use smart home technology, or install a home theater or whole-house audio/visual system, consult with a specialist.

- Custom furniture design – Designers often design and specify custom furniture that is uniquely created just for you. A designer may choose custom finishes, fabrics and trims, or they may design a one-of-a-kind piece. This is a highly specialized skill, and the majority of designers offer this level of service so your interior does not look as if it came from a retail store.

- Purchasing management – Most designers offer this service on a flat fee, "mark-up" or discount from retail basis to cover this time-consuming work that is essential to making sure each piece of your ultimate design puzzle is delivered correctly.

Jennifer L. Markanich, Allied ASID/Steven Long, Photographer

Designers order samples of fabrics from the actual bolts that will be used on your furniture or for your window treatments, bedding and pillows (CFA = Cutting for Approval), to make sure they match the originally selected item. The designer places detailed purchase orders explaining how to apply the fabrics (pattern match and grain) and trims, how to construct and install each item. This takes hours per product. It starts from the time the designer shops, selects items, requests pricing on each component, requests sample finishes and fabrics, creates a proposal, gets your approval, places the order, follows up to make sure the components were delivered to the manufacture or job site, confirms the piece is in production, arranges for shipment, secures insurance in transit, inspects, delivers and installs each piece. Often a unique piece requires specialty drawings with detailed notes to the fabricator, and even visits to the shop floor or job site to make sure the design intent is properly executed. The larger the project, the more time it takes.

Coordinating an entire project with hundreds of components and sometimes hundreds of resources and subcontractors can be overwhelming and takes defined systems, processes and software for a design professional. It is like herding cats. It takes pushing, prodding, begging, sweet-talking and a firm hand to accomplish seeming miracles.

- Project management and scheduling – Interior designers learn most of this on the job, and it takes years to become proficient. A designer that is skilled at project management and scheduling can save you a lot of time and money. It takes many years to develop a strong team that works well together, and that is a great asset that a well-seasoned designer brings to you. A designer normally works with favorite contractors, builders and subcontractors they've used for years because they can rely on them to deal with problems that inevitably arise during projects. Designers protect these resources and do not normally share names unless you hire them for the job. Even if you hire the designer and use their team for a project, it is best if you ask the designer if you may employ these trades for other projects with or without the designer. The designer has spent a great deal of time building relationships and communication processes to ensure you get a great result on time and under budget.

Annie Elliott, Associate ASID/Michael K. Wilkinson for Bossy Color

- Custom drapery design – Some designers specialize in window treatments because it is also highly detailed. This one design element alone can transform your space from blah to spectacular. Understanding how draperies and window treatments are made, what fabrics and trims work in certain installations and how to work with odd-shaped windows is an art. Because window treatments are necessary and also can be expensive, even if you do the majority of the design work yourself, it is worth consulting with a specialist.

- Art, rugs and antiques – A small number of designers are extremely knowledgeable about art, rugs and antiques. Some specialize in particular artists and eras of furniture and can guide you to the best dealers and even shop overseas and assist in designing with wonderful objects for your project.
- Yacht and jet design – Very few designers offer this level of design service. When you need assistance beyond what the yacht or jet manufacturer offers, you will be working with top-tier designers because they work with the most affluent clients who require this type of design.

TOP-TIER DESIGNERS

Top-tier designers are "known brands." Manufacturers seek their endorsement because their name connotes quality. You will typically see them featured in *Architectural Digest*®, *Veranda*™, *House Beautiful*™, *Dwell* and other magazines. A top-tier designer may also be listed in a "Top 100" list for these magazines.

You may also find top-tier designers featured in top blogs and online magazines like *Lonny Magazine*, or they may publish their own blogs, as well. Some designers are also published authors of books, or they may have a TV show either locally or be featured internationally through HGTV.

These top-tier designers are home fashion icons, and they are often sought out by manufacturers to design products or license their name to better sell high-end products.

Linda M. Navara, Allied ASID

Great designers may be found in the larger cities like New York, Los Angeles and Chicago but may also be found in unlikely places in small states. These designers may or may not have an education in interior design, but their style and presence in the interior design world is undisputable.

Having personally interviewed several of these designers for *JustLuxe*, some may seem intimidating, but they aren't. These designers just happen to have amazing skills and talent that makes them style mavens. If you want your home to be done by a top-tier designer, you will find most of them to be friendly, helpful and accommodating.

Annie Elliott, Associate ASID/Michael K. Wilkinson for bossy color

CHAPTER 10

PLANNING YOUR PROJECT —
DO YOUR HOMEWORK

TOOLS

You'll need some tools to get started, and all aspiring interior designers use them.

- Camera (your smart phone will do)
- 25' tape measure
- ¼" graph paper
- Ruler
- Architect's scale
- You can also use an online furniture planning software like http://www.icovia.com/ or http://www.homestyler.com/
- Furniture templates available from most office supply stores
- Your favorite shelter magazines for ideas
- Magazine picture cutter
- Glue stick
- Scissors
- White cover stock paper to adhere your samples
- Notebook dividers
- Plastic sleeves
- Notebook
- Computer with a spreadsheet program like Excel™
- Paint deck

EVALUATE PROFESSIONALLY EXECUTED PROJECTS

Begin your project by looking through design magazines. Purchase 10 or 15 magazines and set aside a day to cut out your favorite pictures. If your partner wants to be involved, encourage him or her to participate in the process, too. If they don't find that process appealing, you can prepare *How To Design Your Perfect Interior Workbook* by "cutting out" your favorite photos, and adhering them to cover stock paper with a glue stick.

If you're the primary design decision maker, you can insert these photos in plastic sleeves and discuss them with your partner. Find out what the other person likes or doesn't like, and why. Write notes in the "Likes and Dislikes" tab of your notebook.

It's just as important to know what you don't like as what you do like. Your list will help you refine and simplify the actual design process.

DOCUMENT YOUR ROOM OR PROJECT

This is where we start as interior designers because we need detailed drawings to ensure that we have the right layout and size furnishings for the space.

Take photos from every angle of the room. Print off your photos if you're using a digital camera, and note which direction your "elevations" (walls) face. If you are unsure, just note the direction of the sun in the morning, since that indicates an eastern elevation. For every elevation, note the direction of the elevation.

Photograph each piece of furniture or major design piece in your room, including art, accessories and rugs. Add these to "My Room Inventory" spreadsheet list. (Go to **www.HowToDesignYourPerfectInterior.com** to download free forms.)

Measure your room floor plan, showing doors and windows. You can use a simple product like Icovia® software to create a plan. Draw the elevations (wall details) showing the location of all doors and windows.

Remember to note where switches, outlets, vents and other important elements are located on the plan.

Stephen Pararo, ASID/Photos courtesy of Pineapple House Interior Design

ANALYZE YOUR CURRENT FURNISHINGS

If you love your sofa, but the fabric is worn, do you want to invest in a new piece, or do you want to reupholster it? The cost for reupholstering can be almost as much as buying new (or even more) depending on the fabric and trims you select. If your sofa is an antique that you love, the investment is worth it.

If your sofa frame is inexpensive and low quality, or the cushioning needs to be refurbished, then it may make sense to donate the item and purchase a new sofa of a higher quality. If you can find a new home for your used item, it is preferable to adding it to the landfill.

Consider how long you want your next sofa to last and that will influence how much you want to invest in the piece. If you plan to keep it for 10 to 15 years, divide the cost by the years you will keep it and compare that to a less expensive sofa you may need to replace in five years. Again, divide the cost by the number of years to get the cost per year for owning that sofa.

Especially if you select a high quality item that is neutral and timeless, it can cost you about the same (or possibly even less) over time, and then you don't have to replace it as often.

If your children are grown, and you are replacing items with higher quality furnishings that you will keep for several years, your decisions will be much different than if you are parents with small children.

Now that you've considered your furnishings, inventory all of your furniture, art, rugs and accessories, measuring first the width, the height and then the depth.

Make notes about what you want to change. If you want to replace, refinish, reupholster or donate an item, add this to the note section of "My Room Inventory" that you can download from **www.HowToDesignYourPerfectInterior.com**.

CREATE A DRAWING OF YOUR SPACE

First measure and sketch your floor plan by hand, or draw it using an online computer software program like Icovia®.

Draw in the furniture items you want to keep and reuse in the space and add those to your floor plan. For example, you may want to use your grandmother's buffet in your dining room, so note its size and location on your plan. Insert other items that you want to add to the space. Try a few layouts to see what works.

Be sure to leave adequate space for circulation and avoid placing items in obvious walkways. It is awkward to walk into the back of a sofa when you enter the room. A more inviting and practical layout may be to turn your sofa 90 degrees so you can walk from the doorway into the middle of the seating area without obstructions.

Stephen Pararo, ASID/Photos courtesy of Pineapple House Interior Design

All seating areas need adequate lighting and tables for drinks, books and accessory items. Make sure each item is proportional to adjacent items.

Allow about 15- to 16-inches between the front of a sofa and a coffee table because you need room to walk. If you plan to purchase a large sectional, you need a large coffee table so it is not dwarfed by the scale of the sectional.

CREATE YOUR WISH LIST

Create the "Design Wish List" spreadsheet (www.HowToDesignYourPerfectInterior.com) of all of the items you would like to include in your project. If you are renovating, many items will be hard to budget for until you complete a drawing that can be given to a subcontractor or vendor for an estimate.

Your room needs a focal point, so decide if it will be a major architectural element like a fireplace, a piece of art or a rug. One of those items may be the starting point for your palette.

If you are redecorating, include any elements you think you want or need for the project. For example, you may want a new sectional sofa, rug, coffee table, end tables, lamps, window treatments, piece of art and some accessories. List those items that you are considering with a budget amount for each item.

If you are not sure what you want to purchase, create a floor plan first using simple graph paper or Icovia® software to try different layouts for your room. Even if you can't draw, you can cut out paper templates for the furniture.

SELECT YOUR PALETTE

There are many ways to select a palette that you like, and the major paint manufacturers even have color combinations you can choose without having to worry about the colors working together because they've done the hard work for you. Even so, it is a good idea to get paint samples and paint them on foam core board (two coats). Look at the boards in daylight and at night with lamps and overhead light. Adding color can be scary, and if you're hiring a painter, it can be costly to paint a space twice.

Design schools teach us how to discern the different components of each color. (That's why it seems so easy for designers to select colors.) For example, a color may include grey, so it is not as intense and clear as a primary color like bright red. Maybe the red you like has a bit of yellow in it. If you can't see the component colors, hire help because the wrong paint color can ruin the effect of the room.

We use this rule of thumb to balance the colors within the room, and you might find it helpful:

Your primary color should make up approximately 60% of the color within your space. 30% can be used for the secondary color and 10% for accents like pillows, accessories, art or even an accent wall. You don't have to follow this exactly, but at least it gives you a suggested guideline.

Take time to make a decision about the paint colors because you want to make sure the color(s) you choose looks good with all fabric and major design elements of the space.

Colors can "shift" when they are placed next to each other, and the quality and type of lighting can affect whether you like the resulting palette in your own home. Never choose a paint color without creating large samples, looking at them next to your fabrics and under your home's light.

Do you love color and want to create drama in your space? Consider using intense colors. If the colors are dark, you can select light colors for upholstery, rugs and window treatments. You will also need additional light in the room. Dark colors make spaces feel close and intimate.

Light colors expand the space. If you want to add color without making it a design element, then use accessories, art and pillows to add a punch of interest.

If you collect or display art, you may want a neutral background so the art stands out. This goes back to deciding on a focal point early in the design process.

SELECT YOUR FURNISHINGS

Shopping online is a great place to start when developing your budget. You still want to sit in the furniture and see if there are local stores where you can see a similar item by the manufacturer you like.

Shopping locally can be advantageous because you can actually talk to someone in person in case of problems. Purchasing items online can be risky because colors don't look the same as they do on your computer screen, and you can't tell anything about the quality of the pieces. Always order samples of the fabric so you can see and feel the quality to ensure it is exactly what you want.

Ask about durability and clean ability, too. You can add finishes to fabric furniture to protect against spills or soiling. This can be done locally.

Take your floor plan with you when you are shopping, as well as a tape measure and a camera (or use your cell phone).

RUGS

The options for all design elements are limitless, so think carefully when investing in rugs because they make an impactful design statement in your room. Rug costs can range from under $100 to hundreds of thousands of dollars for large-scale antiques.

Consider the durability of the construction. A hand-woven or hand-tufted rug will be more expensive and can be more durable than a machine made product, depending on the quality of construction and materials. The quality, colors and finish will vary widely. Since this could be one of the most expensive investments in your space, take your time because you should love it.

Rugs are another complex component of your space and can easily be the most important and expensive focal point for your room. Go here for information about a fabulous book to help you select the best rug for your space.

ART

Since the interior itself is the background for the individually selected treasures of each client, it is more comfortable for designers to stop their work before selecting artwork. Art is something that designers are hesitant to select for their clients because they don't want to impose their taste on what is a very personal decision. Many clients ask for advice about art and artists, and we may have some ideas for you, but ultimately, you should love each piece and take time to acquire what interests you.

Some clients purchase for investment purposes, but unless you are extremely knowledgeable, you should get a referral for an art consultant. If you aspire to get published in major home furnishings magazines, the editors expect you to invest in high end to-the-trade furnishings and well-known artists.

If you like small-scale pieces and you want to put them on a large wall, you can create groupings or add larger scale frames to make the pieces fit the wall scale.

There are few rules regarding art, and if you love contemporary and traditional pieces, there is no reason you can't have both in the same space. Use a unifying theme or color to combine pieces that otherwise might not go together.

Juxtaposing and mixing disparate elements can add interest to your room. Experiment. If you don't like how your first attempt looks, try something else because it is just a few nails and a little bit of spackle and touch-up paint to erase your mistakes.

WINDOW TREATMENTS

Window treatments are one of the most important elements of your space because they frame your views and soften hard edged windows. They can add a luxurious touch and can even become the focal point of your room; however, that is not our preference.

Window treatments are for privacy, protecting your furnishings from sun damage, aesthetics, thermal protection and light control.

There are a few online resources which you can use to order draperies, but they generally work best for simple window configurations. Once you start designing for stacks of windows and patio or French doors, it becomes more challenging to order draperies long-distance without making mistakes.

Even some designers don't tackle draperies because they require a special talent for thinking through details that aren't readily apparent. We rely on the advice of our workroom (fabricator) to prevent expensive mistakes.

If you can't afford to add decorative treatments, start with the privacy needs and sun protection first. You can purchase the basics online or at "big box" stores like Home Depot. Just check the quality before investing. Not all mechanisms are substantial enough to survive heavy use.

Draperies and decorative treatments like cornices or top treatments can transform the look of your room. They will also add considerably to your budget, so they can be added later in the project.

We've seen draperies from retail stores that are supposed to be the same length, and yet when we went to hang them, they weren't even. We've seen draperies with thin cotton lining that look washed out when the sun shines through them. Silk and linen fabrics aren't appropriate for western or southern exposures and may disintegrate in less than a year.

Top quality drapery workrooms use "bump," a felted interlining to create a luxurious feel. However, when you add interlinings, the stack when the draperies are pulled back can overlap more of the window than you intended.

Since drapery construction is complex, it is advisable to seek a professional's assistance because you are investing a great deal of money and you don't want to make expensive mistakes.

Remember the $25,000 set of draperies? That cost was for three windows. That is an extreme example because they were made of Scalamandré silks with hand-made silk trim and tie-backs and tea-stained Scalamandré lace sheers as well as privacy shades.

The client, by the way, loved the elegance and richness of the draperies, and she was delighted with the end result.

Sybil Barrido, ASID/Henry Cabala, Photographer

ACCESSORIES

Accessories add personality to a room like great jewelry adds to an outfit. But over-accessorizing can ruin the elegant design you so carefully created.

Take your time and edit carefully. These pieces can be assembled over time. What you don't want to do is have everything look as if you went to one store and picked all of the items at the same time.

Add items over time and do not over-decorate your space. Less is more.

Scale is important for accessories, too. When you select items for a coffee table, think in triangles and select the tallest item, and the height of the second item should be about two-thirds of the height of that piece, and the third item can be between one third to one half of the height of the first piece. It is a formula that works consistently.

Mix textures and stack items on top of books. Look at your favorite design magazines and see how the top designers accessorize their spaces.

We've shopped overseas for accessories for our clients, and because each piece has a story and the clients know we specifically selected them while traveling, it means more than buying them at Bed, Bath and Beyond® or Pier One®.

It's much better to have no accessories than to purchase poor quality items that don't have personal meaning to you. What makes a room complete is the collected objects that are emotionally connected to a memory like travel, a gift from a special friend (or designer), or family member.

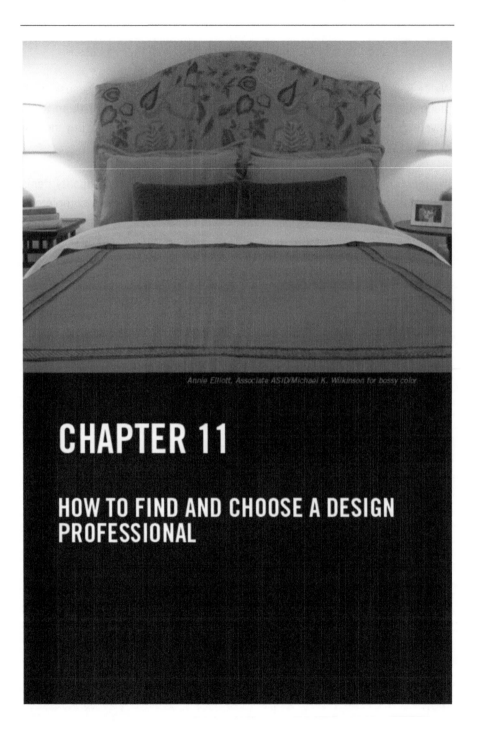

Annie Elliott, Associate ASID/Michael K. Wilkinson for bossy color

CHAPTER 11

HOW TO FIND AND CHOOSE A DESIGN PROFESSIONAL

NOW THAT YOU UNDERSTAND THE DESIGN PROCESS...

Now that your initial thoughts and plans are assembled, depending on the type of project you are considering, you may decide that you need one or more professionals to assist you. It is not unusual to get into the process and find out that it is more work and time than you are willing to invest.

If you are building a house or remodeling, you probably have a good idea of how much you can and are willing to invest in the home or project. It's not that you can't adjust your budget later should you decide to do more or less, but it's a starting place that all members of your team need to honor and work within.

Whatever your budget, set a safety net of 10 percent and deduct that from the amount you share with your design team. Why? Because you may decide that you want to increase the scope or invest more on a few items that might be outside of the original budget. Also, prices can vary, especially if your project will take months or even a few years. It is best to plan conservatively and be prepared for the unexpected.

Often in remodeling projects, your team will give you a proposal based on what can be seen in the space. Once walls are opened, additional conditions may be uncovered and these are generally outside of the scope that was presented.

Your designer will likely ask that anyone that makes financial decisions within the household be present for at least the initial meeting to get an agreement on the scope and investment required for the project. Even though one of you may not want to be involved in the design process, if your partner cares how the money is spent, then you both need to participate in the meetings. It's a sure way to end up with an unhappy relationship if you have conflicts over money.

Judy W. Cody, ASID/Kenn Bird, Photographer

NO-FEE DESIGNERS

Some retail stores provide in-house staff to help you with a furniture plan. They won't necessarily help you with decisions or selections that don't come from their store, unless the clerk works on the side as a designer. That means you need to pull the rest of the room together with paint colors and other items that aren't from that store.

The designer may be on commission, so he or she has an incentive to help you select from only that store. If you like the looks and price points of the store, getting design advice that is included in the cost of your furnishings can be an economical solution for you.

However, if you want a unique, high-end custom interior with the highest quality of construction, buying at retail may not provide the look you really want. And, you may find it challenging to create the result you are envisioning.

There are thousands of interior designers in the United States and abroad, and each one works differently. Because each designer is different in their style, approach, process and fees, you need to decide what you are willing to invest before contacting one for a consultation.

Sticker shock is common when working with a designer for the first time because you may not be thinking of what it costs to provide the creative skills, service and project management to create the desired end result. It is worth some time to educate yourself about your options. The Internet can be a great help.

Hiring a professional does involve an investment, and yet designers can help you acquire high-quality products and services and combine them uniquely to create a one-of-a-kind look. That can be factored into your overall budget. For example, if you purchase a $5,000 sofa and it is the wrong scale and style for the room, then that expense could easily offset the fees that you would have invested with a professional.

Ask people whose homes you admire for the name of their designer. Your Realtor can also make recommendations, and you can look for a designer in a local magazine or newspaper.

Look at the designer's website, and beyond the portfolio, make sure you like the designer's philosophy and "about us" page. You will find great clues to their personality. You must like your designer because the process can take months and sometimes years, so why be unhappy?

WHEN YOU NEED AN ARCHITECT

You need an architect when you are building a home from the ground up, or when you are adding space to your home. It isn't always essential to hire an architect for an interior renovation project unless you are planning to move load-bearing walls. If you live in California in particular, you may need an architect to design for earthquakes.

The role of an architect or an interior designer can overlap when it comes to codes, accessibility and other functional requirements depending on your state. Ask for the professional's opinion about their comfort with the scope of work and if another specialist should be involved.

Interior designers can often design renovation projects and have an architect or engineer review and stamp the plans for permits if moving or removing load-bearing walls is part of the plan. Not all designers do this type of design work, so if your project is extensive, you should ask plenty of questions about the designer's experience with this type of work and decide if you should start with an architect.

WHEN YOU NEED A CONTRACTOR OR BUILDER

Managing a new home building or renovation project is best handled by a licensed general contractor (GC) or builder. The builder or GC has years of experience with a team of subcontractors and vendors. The best ones have a team that they've worked with for years.

If a builder or GC puts things out to bid to new subcontractors on a regular basis, tread carefully because they may be hard to work with, or they may be continually looking for the lowest-priced team to maximize their profits.

Top GCs or builders know that it costs less to have a dependable and reliable team that understands the priorities toward quality workmanship and on-time performance. When the team is constantly changing, it is a red flag and you need to discern what it is telling you.

It is a good idea to visit a prospective GC's or builder's jobsite, because the crew's attitudes will tell you a lot about their relationship with the business owner. Their relationship with their subcontractors is a huge clue about their professionalism and respect for the team.

When a GC or builder doesn't work with the same subcontractors for years, it could also be a sign of financial problems.

What you really want is a team that has experience working together. Even if the bid is slightly more expensive at the beginning, a team with long-term, friendly relationships can actually be less expensive because they are used to solving problems together. There is efficiency of communication that is hard to explain but worth the extra investment.

Maybe you have a burning passion to build and be the contractor for your own home, and if so, then by all means you can do it, but just know that it is a full-time job to manage the process. Not having long-term relationships and accounts with subcontractors and vendors means you will experience trial and error challenges. You can find great resource guides through your library or bookstore.

LICENSING REQUIREMENTS

Currently, 24 states, the District of Columbia and Puerto Rico regulate interior design services. Be sure to review applicable regulations in your state before interviewing an interior designer. Many states have a board that ensures compliance with that state's requirements. The board verifies if an individual is registered, licensed or certified in your state. For a list of states with interior design licensing requirements, go to the ASID website at www.asid.org or call ASID headquarters at (202) 546-3480.

Associations like Designer Society of America provide professional services and a certification program for interior decorators. Decorators may not have

the training to tackle construction projects, so be sure and ask about their experience if you need that type of service.

Most renovation and new construction projects will run more smoothly with the experience of an interior designer that understands the process and manages a team, although a decorator may also do some of this type of work. The lines are often blurred if a decorator has years of self-taught experience in renovation.

If you are interested in restyling or refurnishing your home, an interior designer can also help you with this kind of project, or you can choose an interior decorator. Again, the lines can be blurred between which professional can help you accomplish your goals.

Some design professionals call themselves interior designers in states in which it is allowed even though they have not completed education, experience and NCIDQ® testing. The lines are blurry between an interior designer and interior decorator, and in the case of someone having talent and experience without education and testing, these professionals may use the title, "interior decorator." Even top-tier designers may be decorators and not interior designers though they perform the same services.

Many interior designers have completed a two-, three- or four-year degree in interior design and have up to six years of experience in the industry working for a licensed designer who has completed the NCIDQ® exam. In certain states, they must meet these requirements in order to use the title "interior designer."

Be sure to ask the designer(s) you are interviewing to tell you about their education and experience.

A few designers may also do home staging, which is de-cluttering and de-personalizing your home for sale. Many professional stagers maintain an inventory of furnishings and accessories to style homes and may tackle decorating and not interior design projects.

When you hire someone with education, years of experience, and credentials, it doesn't guarantee a perfect project, but it does provide assurance that you will get the best result possible.

Annie Elliott, Associate ASID/Michael K. Wilkinson for Bossy Color

WHO DO YOU HIRE FIRST?

It's not unusual that the first person who is hired on a project is the interior designer. Why would you do this?

Designers take time to understand how you live and can assess your lifestyle, current furnishings and your future goals. They can recommend how you can design within your current space without adding to your home's footprint to accomplish your vision. You can also hire a designer to consult with you if you are considering purchasing a different home. Furniture plans and discussions about potential renovations can occur before you purchase so you can best evaluate your options.

You may wonder why you would hire an architect as well as a designer for your project. The architect is focused on the shell and functional space, and the designer delves into your lifestyle and preferences in minute detail. That is where the magic happens when the spaces are a perfect blend of both perspectives.

If you're planning a new construction project, and you want your home to perfectly fit your lifestyle, hiring your designer at the beginning of the conceptual process is recommended. Most designers have relationships with builders, general contractors and architects and can give you recommendations for the rest of the team. Once you have a list of names, review their websites to see if their work is appealing to you.

The most important aspect of working with a designer is the relationship.
It takes months and sometimes years to complete a project. Make sure you "click" with the person that is guiding you and helping you invest in your home. Your project will involve thousands of dollars, perhaps hundreds of thousands or even millions if you are building an estate home.

Trust and comfort with the person that helps you make the decisions is crucial. It is important to talk openly and honestly about your budget and your concerns about working with a designer. Communication is the key to a great project.

WHERE DO YOU FIND AN INTERIOR DESIGNER?

Once you have a clear picture of what you want to accomplish and what is important to you, then you are ready to interview three or four designers. You can also find designers by "Googling" for someone in your area. "Interior Designer _____ (your city)" will show you a list of designers nearby.

If you like researching online, you can also find interior designers through the following sites – and this is only a small list of where you can find out about them:

- Yelp
- Angie's List™
- LinkedIn®
- Facebook

- Twitter
- Houzz
- Gilt
- Pinterest

You can also search for "interior design blogs _____ (your city)" to follow top designers in your area.

Some designers offer online "virtual" consultations, workshops both online and at various venues around your metro area, as well as full-service interior design. Today it is extremely easy to work with an out-of-state designer due to the Internet. If you see someone's work you like and they are located across the United States, it is entirely possible to work with them without incurring excessive travel costs.

Referrals are always recommended. Ask your friends, neighbors, Realtor, professional advisors, builders, general contractors, hair stylists, etc. Ask someone who you trust to make a referral. If you hear the same name more than once, you may want to interview that person.

Lola Watson, Allied ASID/Karen Melvin, Photographer

Magazines, both online and print, may include a directory of interior designers, and you can search their online archives to see if the designer has been featured in an article. Some of these listings are given to designers when they advertise in the publication, so the list will not be comprehensive for your area.

Designer showhouses are a great place to see the true creativity of an interior designer because the designer is not restricted by someone else's budget or opinions. Designers often staff their rooms so they can meet you and answer your questions.

Not all interior designers have websites, and in some cases, the site may be minimally populated, because they are busy and may not have invested in a fully featured site. That is changing rapidly, and by the next publication of this book, more will be online.

You can use their online contact form, call or email the designer directly to briefly describe your project. You will want to share the following information:

- Who you are
- How you heard about the designer
- What you like about their work and why you are interested in working with them
- Any questions you might have about their experience, education, certifications, affiliations, etc. that you feel are necessary for your project
- Why you are thinking of hiring a designer
- What your scope of work is
- Where you live (neighborhood)
- Your expected investment in the project
- How do they charge for their services?
- Any deadlines that might affect the project
- Is this a project they would be interested in considering?
- Do they have time for this project?
- Do they have a list of referrals you could send?
- May you contact them?

Tell the designer about other team members you are planning to bring into the project. (If you are planning to assemble a team, a meeting with the possible team members is a great idea prior to hiring each member. Sometimes there can be personality differences and disagreements about roles and responsibilities, so it is a good idea to pick one person to be the "point person" who will work directly with you and decide who has responsibility for each part of the project.)

- Who will be involved in the project and financial decisions on the project
- Whether you are interviewing other designers
- Your timeline for making a decision

Shelley Gorman, Allied ASID/Eric Penrod, Photographer

Depending on the size of the firm, some designers have associates that will talk with you about the project and then set up a time for the principal designer to speak directly with you once they determine if your project and their skills and schedule are a good fit. Both of you are committing to a long-term relationship, so it is a dual decision.

Some designers have an office and a staff, though many work alone from their homes. Others manage a virtual team that may include drafters, renderers, project managers, assistants and a bookkeeper. Some designers don't want the overhead and management responsibility for a team, and they may be equally as qualified as the larger firms to do your project. The solo designers may or may not be less expensive.

After the initial telephone conversation, if you are interested in meeting in-person, some designers prefer to have you come to their studio, the local design center or even a coffee shop to discuss your project and whether you are both interested in taking the next step of having them meet at your home.

The reason most designers prefer to take this interim step is to ensure you are interested in working with them. Most designers do not charge for the "getting to know you" meeting to determine if there is mutual interest.

When a designer meets you at your home, they normally do not offer design ideas until you are ready to go forward with them because it is their intellectual property, and they also need adequate time to think through the entire scope of your project to make well-considered recommendations.

Unfortunately, some consumers believe it is okay to ask for design ideas for free, and then do not hire the designers, nor do they respond and let them know they've decided to do the project themselves or with another designer. It is considered good form to let the designer know if you did not select them and why, so they can learn from the experience. They will appreciate your honesty and will not call or email unnecessarily after that.

Once you are fairly sure you like one designer, a visit to your home is the next step. It does not obligate you to hire the designer, but the designer will want to see the actual space and assess the project scope. Some designers will give you a range of expected fees, a budget range and their retainer policy during that meeting.

Others will assess the project and spend time calculating the budget and fee before meeting with you to review a final letter of agreement and proposal.

Some designers charge for the initial consultation in your home, and some do not. Some will apply it to the total fee. And, if you want design advice during the initial meeting, anticipate that the designer will expect compensation at that time even if you do not proceed with that designer.

A retainer is customary for most projects and can range from a few hundred dollars to many thousand dollars depending on the scope of work. Retainers may be fully applied at the beginning of the project, or half may be held until the end of the project.

Some designers use "evergreen" retainers that are replenished throughout the project. For example, your designer might request a $5,000 retainer and then bill you when the balance falls to $2,500. Your designer may have the right to stop work if you don't replenish your retainer.

The majority of work happens at the beginning of the project, especially if the designer is assisting you with shopping and purchasing. Each proposal takes hours of time to assemble, and much of this work happens behind the scenes. It can be surprising how much time it takes to bring a project together, and to make it all seamless, it takes a lot of detail management.

HOW DO DESIGNERS CHARGE?

When you ask "how do you work?" it means you are asking for the designer's fees. Ethically, designers must tell you how they charge and if they are compensated with commissions from retail or wholesale suppliers even if you pay the source directly. Yet, the designer is not required to tell you their percentage of mark-up.

Other businesses don't share this information, so don't be surprised if the designer doesn't tell you this because it is like asking someone how much money they make.

A designer takes on the liability and responsibility for the order, delivery and installation process in a full-service engagement, and they should be compensated for this service. You want the designer to be profitable and satisfied with their compensation so they do their best work for you.

Somewhere between 50 to 60 percent of the hours spent on your project are for order expediting.

Be sure you trust the designer because they manage thousands of dollars of your money. Remember that you still have control over approving each item's cost and how it fits in your overall budget.

Every designer decides their own billing or fee structure, but the following fee and billing options are the most common:

Hourly only – This may include some or all of these tasks: design, shopping, meetings, drawings, renderings, construction documents, specifications, travel, project management, project scheduling, phone calls to follow-up on projects or discuss the project with you, emails to follow-up on projects or discuss the project with you, and/or administration. If a designer does not make money on managing the purchasing process, their fees may be higher.

- Fees range from under $100 per hour to hundreds of dollars per hour depending on the expertise and brand recognition of the designer. A designer's team members may be billed at lower rates for any of the listed activities. The hourly fee may also be "portal-to-portal," which means they bill from the time they leave and until they return to their office or home.

Hourly + Mark-up – This includes the same hourly information as above, and mark-ups on top of designer wholesale that range from 10 to 100 percent. Some firms do not charge hourly for the administration and instead charge a mark-up on materials, furnishings, services (e.g., carpentry, draperies, picture framing, installation, etc.) to cover their time and company overhead.

Hourly + Discount from Retail – This includes the same hourly information as above, and usually a 5 percent or more discount off of suggested retail. Many retail stores do not offer designer discounts, so when the designers shop at retail with you, they may choose to only charge an hourly fee and/or add a mark-up to cover their time and overhead for managing the ordering, delivery and installation. Some designers will suggest that you pay for the product yourself and arrange for the delivery and installation. Mark-up may also vary depending on the type of product involved.

Hourly + Retail – This includes the same hourly information as above, plus the suggested retail price of the product. The suggested retail is often printed on the tag at a retail store. If you are purchasing from "trade only" showrooms, some manufacturers or showrooms list the suggested retail price. Depending on how the designer charges, if their hourly fees are low, most of their income may be made by selling products. Designers do need to make a mark-up or fee for managing the purchasing process because it is time-consuming. The purchasing function can take as much as 60 percent of their time for a project. Often, the designer will spend significant time resolving problems on your behalf without charging you for this service if you pay a mark-up.

Retail – Very few designers work on a retail-only basis any more. Their fees are based on their experience and expertise. Since you have access to purchase online or at retail without a designer, they could spend a lot of time helping you and not be compensated if ultimately you choose to buy from another source. Some retail stores do not charge for design services and build this into the cost of their products. One way or another, you are paying for design fees. It is not as obvious when purchasing at retail without a fee for the designer's expertise.

Flat Fee or Value-Based Fee – The most experienced designers now offer this method of billing instead of one of the hourly fee options. Typically, the designer uses a cost per square foot ($2 to $50 or more), cost per room ($250 to $5,000 or more), or itemized scope of work with associated costs and profit for their firm (a few hundred dollars for a simple consultation, thousands or even hundreds of thousands of dollars for larger, complex projects), or a percentage of the budget (10 to 30 Percent or more). If the budget expands, you will receive an addendum with a new fee for the revised scope of work. Typically, the number of reselections, job site visits or meetings with you will be limited, and beyond that, you will incur an hourly fee.

- If you tend to be indecisive, the designer may not be willing to work on this basis.
- This allows you to know your investment for the designer's services.
- Some designers also charge a Purchasing Management Fee (often based on a percentage mark-up), and some give you their designer

cost for the purchases. In the latter situation, expect that the fee will be substantially higher.

- Fees can range from a few hundred dollars for a space plan or color consultation, to tens of thousands of dollars for new construction design project from concept to completion. Top-tier designers may charge fees in the hundreds of thousands or even over a million, as appropriate to the scope of the project.

Freight, Delivery, Crating, Inspection, Insurance, Installation and Sales Tax – These fees apply to most purchases. These fees can be 25 percent or more of the item cost. Some designers will bill each of these separately. This can get extremely confusing when you get so many invoices. Some designers will charge a set percentage for all purchases instead of billing you for each separate item.

Travel and Reimbursables – If you are in the same town as the designer, you may not be billed for travel, and if you are billed for travel, it could be per mile, portal-to-portal at the designer's full rate, or half of the designer's hourly rate. If your project requires travel, some designers charge their hourly rate per day or half day, plus the actual costs of the travel plus a small percentage to cover their accounting costs. You may also offer to cover these expenses directly by providing plane tickets and other expenses in advance. Reimbursables may include drawings, renderings, consulting from other experts (architect, engineer, CAD drafter), overnight delivery fees, etc.

Product Payments - Some designers charge in-full for each product they purchase in advance and the orders are non-cancelable once you sign the agreement and provide the payment. This is more efficient for you and the designer and ensures the fastest possible delivery of the products. Some designers will bill a percentage in advance and final amount prior to delivery. It doubles your paperwork and potential confusion when you receive a proposal for part up-front and the rest before delivery. Add the freight, delivery, crating, inspection, insurance, installation and sales tax invoices (all separate) and you can see how overwhelming the paperwork can be when you multiply this by 50 items. You could have 450 pieces of paperwork, not counting monthly statements, instead of 50.

You can tell from all of these options that it is impossible to give you a standard for how designers charge. What is most important is to ask the designer for an expected fee range for a project like yours. The more experienced a designer is the more likely they will be able to estimate the time and expected budget or fee for a project.

Each designer operates their business differently. Most design firms do have substantially more overhead, so expect to pay higher fees. Few designers own shops these days because of the risk and cost of operating them.

Your designer can help you figure out a budget that meets your comfort level and includes their service and design fees. It is common to expect that 10 to 40 percent of the project costs are for creativity, which is the intellectual property (their creative ideas, knowledge and understanding of the intricacies of the process and construction) of the designer that comes from years of experience. Fifty to 60 percent of the fees are for the project and purchasing management services. It takes years to develop well-honed processes, procedures and skills to assist you efficiently.

Stephen Pararo, ASID/Photos courtesy of Pineapple House Interior Design

REFERENCES

It is a good idea to ask for at least three references when hiring anyone to work in your home. Recent references (within the last twelve months) are best.

Here are questions you can ask the references:

- How satisfied were you with the project you did with [potential designer]?

- Were there any surprises?

- Was [potential designer] respectful of your budget?

- Was the project finished on time?

- Was [potential designer] accessible, responsive and responsible?

- Were the details handled to your satisfaction?

- What did you like most about working with [potential designer]

- What did you like least about working with [potential designer]

- Would you use [potential designer] again?

- Is there anything else I should know?

INSURANCE

Many designers maintain Business Owner's Package (BOP) insurance and Worker's Compensation for their team. If they work alone, they may not carry Worker's Compensation insurance.

Not all designers invest in Professional Liability or Errors and Omissions Insurance (these are the same insurance, just different names), but it is recommended, especially if they specialize in construction design.

Designers often take items out on approval, and should carry Inland Insurance to cover any damage or loss of items during transportation to and from your home or while it is in your possession.

If you are remodeling your home, check with your insurance agent to make sure you have adequate coverage and perhaps an Umbrella Policy in case a worker is injured while providing services to you.

Your builder or general contractor should provide proof of Liability Insurance and Worker's Compensation Insurance for their employees. They should also request copies of the subcontractor's Liability Insurance and

Worker's Compensation and call to confirm that the insurance is still in force.

Nitza Shawriyeh, Allied ASID/Krysztof Kociolek, Photographer

CONTRACTS OR LETTERS OF AGREEMENT

It is common practice to sign a Letter of Agreement (contract) that states the terms and conditions of how you work with your designer. It includes how the designer is compensated, how the project is managed, the scope of work, fee structure, what both parties' responsibilities are, what happens if either party doesn't do what they agreed, how the designer is paid and what happens if that does not happen on time, guarantees and warranties that pass to you, the consumer. You and your partner will be asked to sign the agreement.

The agreement should also state what happens if either party wants to terminate the agreement. Some agreements include a mediation or arbitration clause for protection of both parties. Luckily, it is rarely necessary to reach this level of disagreement if you communicate well with your designer. Reasonable people can work through any conflicts or differences without legal action.

Designers retain the copyright and ownership of their design materials and with 100 percent payment of fees, you may use those designs for your project. This includes sample boards, drawings, renderings, sketches, specifications, samples and other work product.

Tere Bresin, ASID, CID/Marisa Pellegrini, Photographer

Designers also ask for the right to photograph your project and use it for marketing, on their website, for publication and public relations outreach. You may decline this request, though it can be fun to see your home in a beautiful shelter magazine. Many times, the publications won't use your name and location (with some exceptions), and this should be discussed in advance with the designer. The designer will pay for the cost of photography, and that may take one to two days depending on the size of your home. You will be asked to sign a release to allow the photography, and you may request a copy of the photographs for your insurance or personal use.

Designers do not proceed without a signed letter of agreement, and you should not expect to receive design concepts or suggestions until you've made this commitment, and most typically with the payment of a retainer because the designer provides intellectual property.

Remember that interior design firms provide a service, and they should be compensated for that. Pay on time because you are working with a small business owner that has expenses, staff and material and labor costs to pay. They are working on your behalf, and when their cash flow is impacted, it affects the delivery of your products and services.

WHEN THINGS GO WRONG ... AND THEY DO

Here is what can happen outside of the designer's control. A few examples include:

- A vendor goes out of business
- Products are discontinued
- Shippers lose items in transit
- Items are damaged in transit or during delivery
- Someone on the team makes a mistake
- Subcontractors, contractor, builder, installers or employees don't show up
- Collateral damage happens during an installation
- Products don't work
- You and your partner don't agree about expenditures or selections
- You or your partner are indecisive

Your designer will assist you to resolve these problems, so let them know what is bothering you as quickly as possible.

Perhaps the designer is busy, ill or forgets to take care of something. Assume good intent first and ask them to address any issue as soon as possible.

YOU CHANGE YOUR MIND

If you signed an agreement or proposal and you decide you don't want to go forward, it may be too late to do anything because custom furnishings are exactly that .... made to order. On rare occasions, the designer may be able to return the item with a restocking fee, and yet in most cases, it is yours. That is why it is important to understand what you're ordering before signing the agreement and providing payment.

YOUR DESIGNER DOESN'T LISTEN TO YOU OR DOES SOMETHING YOU DON'T LIKE

You can terminate your agreement with the designer once you've paid for the items you've agreed to order, including their time. Sometimes it doesn't work out, so just end it quickly.

If you are concerned about costs or selections, say so immediately and ask for less expensive alternatives. Ultimately, what you spend and choose is at your discretion. Do not feel forced to make decisions that are not comfortable to you.

YOUR TRAVEL, PERSONAL OR BUSINESS SCHEDULE IS EXCESSIVELY DEMANDING

Your design professional needs timely decisions and payments to move your project forward, so if you are extremely busy, be aware that your job may suffer. Designers will try to accommodate your schedule, and if online meetings are an option during work hours or lunch time, that is generally preferred because they also have busy schedules and outside obligations.

Some designers charge higher fees if it is not possible to meet during normal business hours. They will do their best to have organized materials and presentations to minimize your time involvement. Some design firms use cloud-based software programs that allow you to access your account information 24/7 so you can make decisions when it is convenient to you.

YOU ARE ANXIOUS ABOUT YOUR DECISIONS

It's common to rethink a few decisions, and if you wake up in the middle of the night with a concern, please remember that few designers respond to emails, calls or text messages after business hours because of personal obligations. Send an email or text and allow enough time for the designer to get back to you. Patience is recommended for your sanity and theirs.

IF YOU AND YOUR PARTNER DON'T AGREE

Remodeling and construction projects can create a tremendous amount of stress if you have different taste, different values about money and design, or conflicts outside of the design project itself. Designers are good about helping you find a design decision that works for both of you, but they are not marriage counselors. Just remember that if you agree on 80 to 90 percent of all decisions and each of you has a win or two, it is a good thing. Be willing to compromise. It is design, and not life and death.

IF YOU ARE INDECISIVE

Be honest with your designer and let them know you have difficulty making decisions before the project starts. It is not fair to go into a fixed or value-based fee agreement if you expect the designer to keep giving you options because you're afraid of making a final decision. Your designer is there to help you make the best possible decisions, and often, you need to trust their advice because that is why you hired the designer in the first place. If something doesn't seem right, or is truly bothering you, please say so. The designer cannot read your mind.

Take time to consider your decisions, and if you have found strategies to help you through the decision process for other projects, be sure to share that with the designer.

COMMUNICATION

Communication is critical when working with a designer. It is a two-way street. If you need more information, be sure to say so. Be available and make decisions as quickly as you can without allowing yourself to feel rushed. Return calls, texts or emails and remember, the latter two methods may not convey your intent. Carefully consider how you write your messages so they are not harsh or demanding.

If the designer is not responsive enough, be sure to let him or her know.

Annie Elliott, Associate ASID/Michael K. Wilkinson for Bossy Color

UNMET EXPECTATIONS

Don't assume that your designer knows that you have specific preferences (such as daily cleaning because of dust, for instance) or that you think the process should proceed in a certain way.

If you don't want calls during certain times of the day, evening or weekend, or you prefer to be emailed or texted rather than called, let the designer know.

Designers, on the whole, are great mind-readers because they work hard to understand what you don't say as much as what you do say. You will likely find it easy to trust your designer to be understanding and supportive because listening and understanding your real motivations and what makes you tick helps them serve you better.

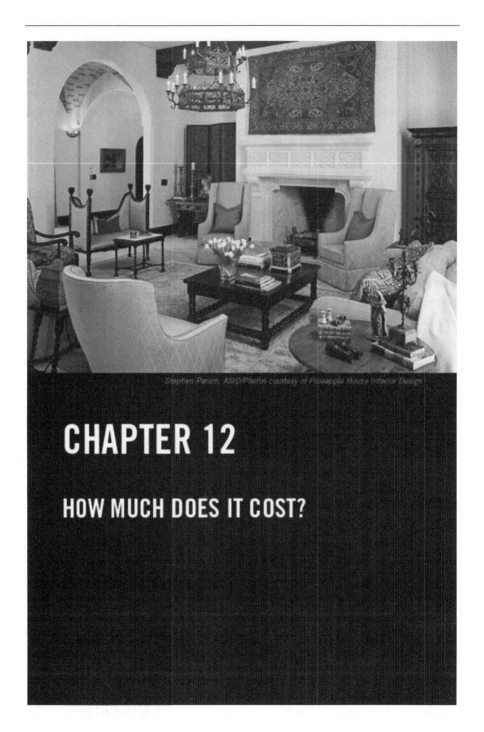

Stephan Pararo, ASID/Photos courtesy of Pineapple House Interior Design

CHAPTER 12

HOW MUCH DOES IT COST?

An experienced designer can give you a good idea of a reasonable budget based on similar projects. Perhaps you are remodeling, and based on your scope and taste, the designer can show you a similar project and the costs for that. Of course your project will be different, but it will give you a frame of reference.

If you're refurnishing, ask about the cost of some of the projects in the designer's portfolio. You're not expected to know what it costs to create a particular room, but you do know how much you're willing to spend. Within that, the designer should be able to guide you to establish a reasonable budget.

Shelley Brose, Allied ASID/Martin King of Laguna Beach, Photographer

HOW TO SET YOUR BUDGET

If you have been in your home for years and haven't remodeled or refurnished since you moved in, then you need to prepare yourself for the investment it requires to bring your home up to date.

Your budget could be determined by the savings you've put aside to redo your kitchen or master suite. If so, take some time to shop at retail stores or online to get a sense of what things cost.

Shelley Brose, Allied ASID/Martin King of Laguna Beach, Photographer

Click here http://www.remodeling.hw.net/facts-and-figures/cost-vs-value-report/ to get the most recent report about national averages for typical room remodels.

If you're redecorating, it is important to look at the resources you have access to online or in your city to determine pricing. A sofa can range from a few hundred dollars for a low quality one, to $3,000 to $5,000 for a moderately priced sectional, or even $20,000 and up for a custom "designer" sofa.

Tere Bresin, ASID, CID/Daniel Eifert, Photographer

Rugs range from under $100 for acrylic fiber available at big box stores to $1,500 to $5,000 for a mid-range rug to $100,000+ for an antique oriental.

Window treatments can be purchased online (construction is low-quality with inexpensive cotton lining, no interlining and machine stitching; the lengths can vary per panel), to $1,500 to $5,000 for simple store-bought panels constructed of silk with hardware, to more than $10,000 per window for multiple layers of window treatments. For example, if your fabric is a fine designer fabric with lining and interlining, hand-made trim, lace sheers, top treatment with trim, and a privacy blind, you can achieve a one-of-a-kind look that lasts for years. Don't forget that you need to count the number of windows you have in a room and multiply it with the cost per window. Window treatments can be expensive, and yet they provide privacy, beauty, light control and protect your furnishings, so it is important to be prepared financially for this investment.

When you are investing in custom draperies, it pays to hire a professional to assist you. Any errors can be extremely costly. A professional that specializes in window treatments understands construction, appropriate materials for the application and how they are installed. It takes a tremendous amount of knowledge to do a great job at window treatment design. The quality of the workroom and the installer is also critical to the ultimate result.

Chandeliers can be simple metal and range from a few hundred dollars to a few thousand dollars for a moderately priced fixture. The high-end of chandeliers (for instance, those from Schonbek with crystals) can be many thousand dollars.

Antiques vary in cost by city and will definitely add thousands of dollars to your budget.

If you are looking for inexpensive prints for your walls, you can find them at retail starting at under $100 for giclées (fine art digital prints made on ink-jet printers) of lesser known artists' work for a few hundred dollars to thousands of dollars. Serious art pieces start at a few thousand dollars for small pieces and may be many thousands for larger or rarer works.

You can start your budget by making a spreadsheet of what you think you want to have in your room and then list the costs per item to give you a starting point for your budget.

If your entire budget for a room is under $5,000, you can get some online advice from a design website, but most likely, you will want to do most of the work yourself.

Steffany Hollingsworth, ASID/Katie Johnson, Photographer

If you need a starting point to set a budget, you can also use a percentage of what you invested in your home. For example, if you paid $500,000 for your home and you are planning to do a moderate refurnishing job, 10 percent of that amount is a bare minimum. If you are starting from scratch, you can spend at least 20 to 50 percent of the cost of your home to refurnish and remodel. Only you know what is comfortable to you.

The design shows on TV are entertaining, but set unrealistic expectations about the speed and cost of projects. They do not factor in the planning time, which can take months and involve a large team of professionals, designer's fees, subcontractor's and contractor's fees, or materials costs (which are often donated by program sponsors or advertisers).

Designers also don't compete by providing free design concepts to get your project. That is a media myth.

Designers provide extensive knowledge and creativity and expect to be compensated fairly for their services. If you know your budget is small, then try to do the work yourself, or save up to create a one-of-a-kind project.

Claudia Panizza, Allied ASID/Melabee Miller, Photographer

WHAT SHOULD I EXPECT TO PAY A DESIGNER?

A designer's fees (not including markup on products) can range from 10 to 40 percent (or more) of your renovation or refurnishing budget. If your budget is on the low end, the percentages will be higher and vice versa.

If the designer charges an hourly fee, it is rare to find anyone working for less than $50 to $100 per hour. The mid-range is $101 to $200 per hour, and top-tier designers are in the over $200 range.

Some retail stores offer design services, and they are often included in the purchase you make, but they are limited to furniture plans using furniture from the store and some of your own items. The rest of the project is up to you, unless the designer works outside of the store.

As mentioned, fees are dependent on the designer's expertise, credentials, creativity, brand, years of experience, and the typical market rate in your area. We only provide these ranges so you have some sense of where to start.

HOW TO MANAGE YOUR BUDGET

Once you create a realistic budget for yourself, decide how you will handle the situation if you or your partner/spouse want to spend more than you agreed initially. Agree on the limit of what you can decide without discussing it with the other person.

Talk to your banker before you start designing your project if you need a loan. You don't want to finish the design and find out that the bank will not make the loan.

Don't spend more than you can comfortably afford, or over-improve for your neighborhood, unless you are willing to pay extra for your personal enjoyment. It's not worth the stress of extra credit card debt if you are stretched too tight or losing thousands of dollars if you decide to move in less than five years.

Since home values are so much lower today, go into your project knowing it is unlikely that you will get 100 percent of your investment back in the remodel. You need to make a value decision about whether it makes sense because you love your home, location and neighbors, you don't like change, or you don't want to uproot your kids and move out of your school district.

If you are unsure about whether you should do a remodel, talk to a local Realtor. Sometimes it makes sense to move to a different house if your project will over-improve your home for your neighborhood.

Your budget is important and it is essential that you trust your design professional with your financial limits. You know how much you are willing to invest. You may not know how much you can get for that limit, but you do know what is comfortable to you.

Your designer can help you establish a reasonable plan and can "value engineer" the design to accomplish your goals whether your taste and budget lead you to shop at IKEA® with a little advice or a master plan, or invest in a completely custom solution.

One seasoned designer recommends setting aside a credit card with a specific limit or a separate bank account for your project. Once you do that, your decision is made and that should be shared openly with your interior designer.

A good designer will not exceed your budget unless you change your mind and decide to expand the scope of work and what you are willing to invest. When you maintain a 10 percent buffer account beyond what you tell your designer and construction team, you'll cover yourself in case you add to the scope or additional expenses from unforeseen circumstances arise (behind-the-wall expenses like plumbing or additional building code updates).

WHEN DOES "SAVING MONEY" BY DOING IT YOURSELF REALLY COST YOU MONEY?

If you don't feel confident with your design eye, then think about the budget parameters listed earlier in the book. If you make a mistake on the scale of a sofa, or you select material that isn't appropriate, the mistake can cost you thousands of dollars.

If you hire a painter to paint a room, it could cost $500 to $5,000, and if the paint color doesn't look good with everything else, you could end up paying the price to repaint at least one more time.

If you are painting your own room, then it only costs a few cans of paint—around $100. Decide what you're willing to risk on mistakes and factor that into your plans.

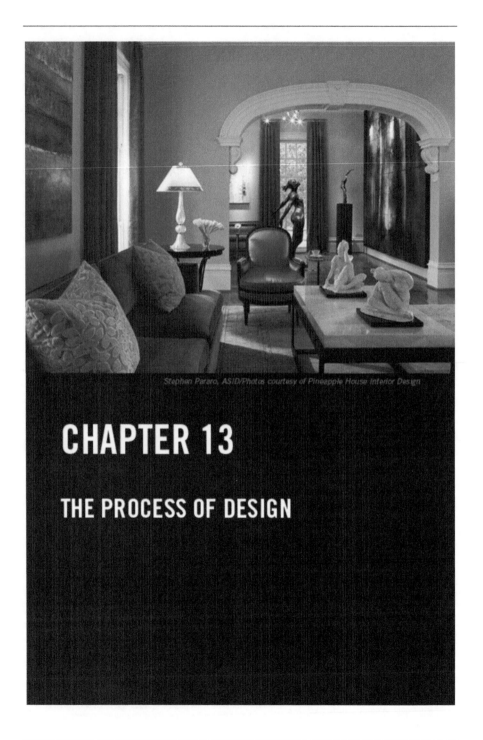

Stephen Pararo, ASID/Photos courtesy of Pineapple House Interior Design

CHAPTER 13

THE PROCESS OF DESIGN

WHAT TO EXPECT

Expect some unknowns, especially if you haven't previously done the type of project you are tackling. Stay relaxed and flexible, if possible, because it will reduce your stress level.

Assume that everyone on your project has good intentions unless you see evidence that tells you otherwise.

Don't surprise your partner with hidden spending or scope creep due to your taste being more expensive than what you agreed to spend. That's why designers prefer to have both of you present during the planning process because both of you do care about the money you invest, and you don't want to have marital problems as a result.

If you are doing your own shopping, design and labor, allow plenty of time to create your *How To Design Your Perfect Interior Workbook* and to do your research. It can take months. It can be a fun process, and sometimes it can be frustrating, too.

HOW LONG DOES IT TAKE?

It can take months to plan your project yourself, and if you work with a designer, it can depend on the designer's current client load. If you have a specific deadline in mind that is non-negotiable, and if your preferred designer can't meet the dates, then you either need to postpone the project or select a different designer.

If you are building or remodeling, the planning part can take as long as the construction. If you are doing a kitchen remodel, it will take a minimum of twelve weeks and sometimes as much as six months from beginning to end. Your job will go faster if all materials are on-site before the demolition begins. Cabinets can take four to 24 weeks to produce, depending on the level of customization. They should be selected right after you select your appliances.

If you are redecorating and working with a designer, custom furnishings with to-the-trade fabrics and trims can take 12 to 16 weeks or longer. The ordering process is somewhat tedious and takes hours to manage. After you sign off on your proposal, the designer places a purchase order for each component and requests CFAs to match them to the original samples to make sure the color, quality and texture match.

Once all fabric and trim CFAs are approved, the fabrics and trims are shipped to the manufacturer. The designer follows up to make sure that all components made it to the manufacturer and then gets an estimated completion date. Manufacturers do not start constructing a piece until all components are there.

Once the piece is ready to ship, it will be placed on a truck. It can be shipped separately for a higher price or shipped with a half or full load. It can take up to two weeks to arrive at the receiver's dock, who will then notify the designer that the product is in town. The designer will inspect the item before delivery to make sure there is no damage and then arrange for delivery to your home.

One July, a client ordered a sofa with multiple fabrics and trims for the pillows. We kept checking the status and one fabric just didn't arrive. Finally, after three months, the vendor told us that the fabric manufacturer "would make the fabric," but they were in financial trouble. We scrambled to reselect another fabric, and we second-day aired the fabric to the manufacturer.

By this time, the client was worried that the sofa would not arrive by Thanksgiving. She was right to be concerned. The manufacturer was swamped with orders due before Christmas and told us that the sofa wouldn't be ready to ship until the week before Christmas, and because the freight companies were so busy delivering orders for the holiday, it was unlikely the sofa would arrive until the beginning of the next year. The client was understandably upset because she wanted to have all of her family sitting on the sofa to open their presents. We didn't want to disappoint her, so we "FedEx®ed" the sofa, and begged the receiver to deliver on Christmas Eve. We absorbed the extra freight charge, and the client was thrilled that her holiday vision was realized.

WHAT HAPPENS WHEN SOMETHING GOES WRONG?

Stay calm and remember it isn't life threatening. It may be frustrating to deal with delays or the multitude of things that can go wrong, but everything that is done for your home is dependent on lots of people doing their job right and following up on the details.

A Dallas client invested in a "bench made" (hand-carved) Karges custom chair with a black lacquer finish and Donghia silk fabric—a $5,000 investment in the late 1990s. From the time she accepted the proposal, we placed the purchase order, second-day aired the CFA, approved the CFA, ordered the fabric, and 20 weeks later, the chair shipped. We waited the typical two weeks and checked on the order. It never arrived at the receiver (the company that accepts the truck, inspects and delivers to the client's home). We filed a freight claim and re-ordered the chair. The second time it actually arrived —18 weeks later. It took 38 weeks to receive the chair. The client still loves the chair to this day; it is the focal point of her home's entry.

If you're doing your own project, keep detailed notes about your conversations. Email trails are very helpful, so get everything in writing.

If you're working with a design professional, let him or her know if you're concerned about anything, and say so immediately when you are ready to discuss it calmly. Keep a running list of questions and discuss those at least weekly. It's better to have a regular communication time set up so you're not overwhelming the design professional with lots of emails, texts or calls.

Our Dallas high-rise client ordered a custom sectional sofa. Our project designer found a fabulous Manuel Canovas white-on-white fabric that looked like coral (she grew up in Sarasota, Florida, so this selection was a huge hit). Two fabric CFAs arrived from Italy, and it was clear that the two pieces were not from the same dye lot. We checked with our vendor, and because we rejected the CFAs, we had to wait for the fabric to be loomed after the typical one month holiday in Italy. We kept the order in place and looked for an entire month for alternatives. She didn't like anything as well.

We told her she should wait for her original selection even though she didn't have a sofa to sit on. Finally, the sectional arrived just in time for her Thanksgiving party to celebrate her new home. It took six months to receive the furniture, and to this day, she has it cleaned regularly and still loves it.

If you're unhappy about fees, don't slow pay or avoid paying the bill. Call and discuss it directly with your design professional immediately. Otherwise your work could be stopped, you could face finance charges, or even worse, legal action because you have signed a legal agreement. Open communication is important.

If you follow the recommendations we outlined, you are unlikely to encounter problems with your designer. However, if a problem arises, there are agencies that can help. If your state has interior design regulations, you can contact the board or agency that monitors compliance. If your state currently does not regulate interior design, contact the department of consumer affairs or consumer protection.

All members of ASID agree to abide by the Society's Code of Ethics and Professional Conduct. If you believe an ASID member has behaved unethically, please contact the ethics coordinator in the government and public affairs department at ASID headquarters at gpa@asid.org, or by phone at 202.546.3480.

WHAT ARE MY RESPONSIBILITIES WHEN I WORK WITH A DESIGN PROFESSIONAL

Communicate openly and honestly with anyone you're working with throughout your design process. If you and your partner are not in agreement, ask your point-person to help you resolve the challenge. They are skilled at working with couples to help them through the process. The "good cop, bad cop" situation occurs occasionally and it makes the process uncomfortable and unproductive. Please don't put your design professional in the middle.

Make decisions as quickly as you can because it moves the process along more efficiently. If you need more information, request it as soon as possible and let the team know you're struggling with the decision. Maybe they can help.

One client said during an initial interview that she struggled to make decisions and needed "hand holding." She agonized over each decision, and because she paid hourly, it was not a financial hardship for our firm, but it was expensive for her, and yet she was willing to invest in the design therapy. She loved the results, but every single one was painful for her because she was afraid of making mistakes.

Process the paperwork, including signing proposals, and provide payments promptly and as agreed. It moves the process forward quickly.

Remember to refer your design professional if he or she does a great job. It is mostly a referral business and they work very hard for you.

Stephen Pararo, ASID/Photos courtesy of Pineapple House Interior Design

CHAPTER 14

HOW TO RELAX AND ENJOY THE PROCESS

Design can be a lot of fun, and yet, when you're making expensive decisions, it makes the calmest person tense and irritable.

TIPS TO SURVIVE A REMODEL

Remodeling is stressful, and if you can move out during the process, it is advisable. This must be factored into your budget. Pack up anything in the areas to be remodeled and move it off-site or to a storage container during the process.

It could lead to a massive clean-out of your basement, garage or attic, and that can be cathartic but also time-consuming. Make sure you have plenty of time to do this outside of work and personal activities.

Start this process early—and if you can do it as soon as you start designing, it will be done by the time the project is ready to begin.

If you are working with a builder or general contractor, they will have a process in place to manage your project. You want to ask lots of questions so you're as prepared as possible. Preparation and knowledge are essential.

Be sure to ask what you can do to help the project go smoothly. Your first project is always the hardest because the disruption in your life is bigger than you can imagine.

REALISTIC DEADLINES

If you have a special event coming up like a graduation or wedding and you want to have your home done before it, make sure you start at least six months ahead if it is a minor refresh, or 12 to 18 months ahead if you are planning to remodel. Rushing contributes to mistakes and ends up costing more money in the end.

PHOBIAS AND IRRITATIONS

Construction generates dust. If you hate dust and you are planning to remodel, tell the designer in advance so that the project scope includes extra cleaning, or arrange with your own housekeeper or cleaning service to keep up with it.

During a kitchen facelift that involved a small amount of carpentry and painting, when we visited the jobsite one afternoon, our client told us she was terrified that when her husband came home he would be furious that there was dust in the house. The crew was exceptionally clean, so it never occurred to me that this would be a problem. She was very upset. We called a friend with a concierge business and got a crew of 10 people to come in and clean the house before he arrived. The cleaning crew arrived within two hours, worked for four hours, and the final bill was $1,000.

If you don't want subcontractors at your home before or after a certain time of day, or you are uncomfortable with the subcontractors being in the home with your children, be sure to tell the designer.

If you don't want tools, drop cloths or materials for projects visible when the workers aren't there, say so. These preferences can be accommodated but could add to your project costs because of the extra time involved.

One client was quite upset because the shutter crew staged shutter panels in each room even though they could not install the shutters in one day. She thought they should only bring in what they could install each day. It was too late by the time we received the call to reach the shutter company to remove the panels. The next day and until the installers finished the job, they had to bring in just what they could put in by the end of the day. It never occurred to us that this would be a problem, but it bothered the client.

SECURITY

Discuss security with the contractor and with your insurance agent. Dumpsters, construction trucks and portable toilets alert thieves that great items are available, so if you aren't staying on-site during the project, make sure your contractor sets the alarm every day and secures the materials in a safe place, such as the garage or inside your home. Thieves love to get into storage trailers, especially if they think they can find tools, appliances or other valuable items.

During a $4.6 million spec house project, the millwork crew left a large trailer with $40,000 of equipment on-site. Thieves broke the padlock and stole everything. It took weeks for the millwork company to replace their equipment, and the job took more time as a result.

Notify your alarm company about your project. If you have an alarm system, give a separate code to the contractor and each of the subs and show them how to use the system.

On one full remodeling project, the client lived in another state. We were in charge of the entire project, and on at least a dozen occasions, the alarm went off and we had to check the jobsite at random hours on the weekends and in the evenings. The client was irritable. We finally figured out that water was leaking under the low windows in the family room and shorting the alarm wires. The client decided to replace the windows. Everything was fine again .... until the alarm went off one early morning. We went to the jobsite to check, and the drywall subcontractor was calmly working. He said that he couldn't get the alarm to turn off. We asked him what code he used, and he said, "KAT." It was supposed to be "CAT." It happened a second time with the air conditioner installer, and he told us the same thing. The client was annoyed, and then amused.

Have someone check the premises at the end of each day to make sure the property is secure. Ask your neighbors to keep an eye on your property if you vacate your house during the project, and have them notify the police if any strange vehicles are there on the weekends or evenings.

Notify your local police station about your remodel. It doesn't guarantee they will patrol more often, but it doesn't hurt to let them know.

Remove valuables from your home. Even though your contractor and subcontractors are nice and seem responsible and trustworthy, doors and windows can be left open, and people can slip in during breaks when the workers aren't in every room. Store any personal papers and account information in locked files—preferably off-site.

One renovation project we undertook was for a client that lived out of town. We told them to remove all valuables during the project. When the client moved in, she was panicked because her mother's mink stole (very sentimental to her) was missing. We remembered that we told her specifically to remove items, and she finally realized she gave it to her housekeeper for safekeeping.

Put motion detector lights around your property to protect your perimeters. Make sure the builder has a checklist on the exit door to turn off lights, lock windows and doors, and set the alarm. Notify your alarm company if you are doing work on your home.

During the remodel of our next door neighbor's home, my husband was reading the Sunday newspaper in the back yard and noticed a white van pull up in the back of their home. He didn't think anything of it because he thought it was someone from the normal crew. The next day, the builder arrived to find that the bathroom vanity cabinets were gone. His insurance replaced them, but it slowed down the job.

SET UP TEMPORARY SPACES SO YOUR FAMILY CAN FUNCTION

If you stay in your home during a remodel, especially for your kitchen, talk with your contractor and designer about setting up a mini kitchen during this time. If you have a space for your current refrigerator, cabinets and a countertop, the items that are removed from your current kitchen can be used throughout the project. If you can prepare meals and freeze them prior to the project, it will make it much easier for you and your family. Make sure the temporary kitchen is not in an area where materials need to be stored.

CONSTRUCTION HOURS AND NOISE

Workers tend to start early, and unless you are in a high-rise building that restricts hours, you want to prepare your family for early arrivals—as early as 7 a.m. If that is unacceptable, let the general contractor know. If you don't want work to be done on the weekend, let the contractor know, and be respectful of your neighbors.

Let the contractor know in advance and make sure you discuss your expectations for jobsite cleanliness and safety.

Set expectations for behavior on site: Don't use the refrigerator or inside bathrooms, clean up after yourself, remove trash daily, radios to be turned down low (or none if preferred), no work between x hour and y hour. No smoking, drinking or cursing in the house.

STAGING OF TOOLS AND MATERIALS

Typically you want to move your vehicles out of the garage and driveway during your project. The contractor will need space for saws and materials.

CONTRACTOR ETIQUETTE

Ask your contractor when it is okay for you to walk through the job site. They are concerned for your safety and disruptions during the project, and it could be inconvenient for you to walk through the project if he is with his team.

Don't micromanage the project if you're working with a team of professionals. Speak up if you're concerned, but let your contractor do his or her job. If you're curious about why something is being done, talk to your contractor or builder.

Do not speak directly with the subcontractors about it.

COMMUNICATION IS CRUCIAL

If you are concerned about something on your project, talk to your designer or contractor, whichever person is your point-person. Don't discuss issues directly with the subcontractors because they report directly to the contractor. They do not have the authority to make changes without the contractor's express direction because they have a contract directly with him or her.

Susan Lobalzo, ASID/Lew Stamp, Photographer

HOW TO KEEP YOUR CREW HAPPY

It is a great idea to buy pizza or sandwiches occasionally for the crews. They appreciate it and will work even harder for you.

KEEP YOUR NEIGHBORS HAPPY

Alert your neighbors about your upcoming remodeling project. A nice gift certificate for dinner would be a great touch before and after the project, and you can even give them a before, during and after tour. Many great neighbors will get frustrated with remodeling debris, subcontractor trucks, deliveries, strange workers, dumpsters and portable toilets outside of your home. Keep the exterior of your home clean and have the dumpster covered each day if possible.

Think about where the dumpster and portable toilet should be located. The weight can damage your driveway, so if it makes more sense to place it on the street in front of your home, plan for that. The city may require a permit.

If you are in a high-rise, condominium, townhouse or covenant-controlled community, check for restrictions or by-laws that might affect your design decisions or project process.

Susan Lobalzo, ASID/Lew Stamp, Photographer

KEEP PETS AND CHILDREN AWAY FROM THE PROJECT

It is best to keep pets and children out of the way of construction areas. Pets become stressed with construction projects, and if they are older, it can be too much for them. If you can have someone else take care of the pets during a project, it is preferable. Children should be kept out of these areas because the tools and equipment can be dangerous.

Shelley Gorman, Allied ASID/Eric Penrod, Photographer

TIMING

Plan for your daily activities to take longer; and just remember, this too shall pass. The temporary inconvenience is worth the end result. If you use a design professional, you can invest in a rendering of the finished space so you can post it where you can see it. Focus on the finished project and not the noise, dust and disruption.

Plan your vacation during the demolition part of the project if you can, and be sure your contractor and subs have your cell phone number and a back-up contact in case of emergency.

If you are remodeling your kitchen, summertime is a great time to do your project because you can grill outside and use your patio furniture for dining al fresco.

Sybil Barrido, ASID/Henry Cabala, Photographer

BUDGET CONTROL

We talked earlier about setting extra money aside in case you add to your scope or unforeseen things affect your original plans. You can put this in a separate bank account from the project funds which should be separate from your household funds because it can be unnerving to see thousands of dollars go out of your checking account in big chunks.

"WHILE YOU'RE AT IT ..."

This is one of the most common problems that happens on jobs and can lead to misunderstandings and conflict. If you add to the scope during the middle of the project, know that the designer and construction team will bill you for additional services and products. It will affect your budget and your project schedule.

If you are remodeling or building, that one dreaded phrase can cause change orders that delay the project and cost extra because the builder, contractor or designer must make accommodations for the changes. It can cause a domino effect because one seemingly small change may result in all of the trades needing to be rescheduled, and that is why it costs extra to use change orders.

CHANGE ORDERS

Remember that changes in the middle of the project can completely disrupt the contractor's schedule and can cause a tremendous amount of frustration and delay as well as additional costs.

A well-designed project addresses all possible thoughts that might arise, but of course, it is not a perfect world. Just understand that those words will ultimately cost you more money and time. Don't expect the designer or construction team to absorb those extra costs.

It's best to start a new project after your first job is close to completion if you want to remodel or redesign another area of your home. You can discuss it with your designer and contractor so you're ready to start once the first part is done. This often happens when you're in the middle of one project and you see how amazing the project is.

Stephan Pararo, ASiD/Photos courtesy of Pineapple House Interior Design

CHAPTER 15

LOOKING FORWARD

You've now prepared yourself to "design your perfect interior," and you know what to expect. Most importantly, you have made decisions about your priorities and you know what it takes to design and complete your project.

You are excited and nervous at the same time, and that is normal. Just remember that you took the time to plan, and that will pay off in lower costs and higher satisfaction.

We shared the big myths and "secrets" which were really unspoken truths about the profession of interior design. Just remember that you can and will have a beautiful home. It may take you longer and cost more money than you initially expected, but if you complete the exercises you will be prepared.

Enjoy the process and "don't sweat the small stuff." Your home will soon be magazine-perfect.

What really matters is how you feel when your project is complete, after the dust has settled. Ultimately, your home is the place where you feel settled, relaxed, comfortable and calm so you can live each day with happiness and ease. That is not a luxury, it is a necessity.

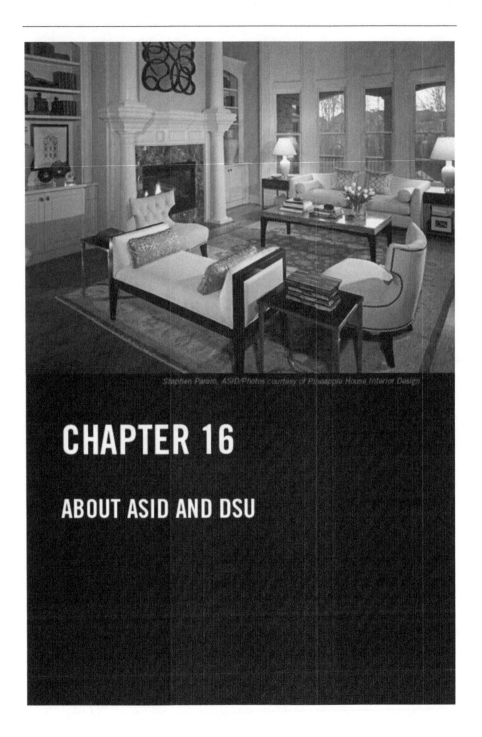

Stephen Param, ASID/Photos courtesy of Pineapple House Interior Design

CHAPTER 16

ABOUT ASID AND DSU

AMERICAN
SOCIETY OF
INTERIOR
DESIGNERS

Founded in 1975, the American Society of Interior Designers is the oldest, largest and leading professional organization for interior designers. _The History of ASID: 30 Years of Advancing the Interior Design Profession_ was published in 2005 to commemorate the Society's extensive achievements.

ASID has more than 16,000 interior design practitioner members located in all 50 states, the District of Columbia and Puerto Rico.

When you hire an ASID member, you get an experienced practitioner that can solve problems, help you avoid costly mistakes, and most importantly, create an attractive, affordable space designed specifically for you.

ASID members have the training and expertise to manage all of your project's details. They understand the importance of listening carefully to your ideas and needs. From consultation to planning the finishing touches, your ASID professional designer can help you every step of the way by offering options and working within your budget.

ASID offers members continuing education opportunities about appropriate materials, technology, building codes, government regulations, health and safety standards, design psychology and product performance.

All members must agree to abide by the Society's Code of Ethics and Professional Conduct to maintain their membership.

To locate a qualified ASID designer to help you with your project, visit the ASID Referral Service (Find a Designer) at **https://member.asid.org/asidssa/rflssareferral.query page**, or call ASID headquarters at (202) 546-3480.

WHAT THE ASID APPELLATION MEANS

ASID interior designers have the education, training and expertise to manage all the details of your project. They know the importance of listening to your ideas and understanding your needs. From consultation to planning to the finishing touches, they can help you every step of the way, augmenting your choices and adding value to your budget.

All ASID interior designer members must meet basic educational and professional qualifications and agree to abide by the ASID Code of Ethics and Professional Conduct. Many have also passed a professional qualifying examination administered by the National Council for Interior Design Qualification (NCIDQ). In addition to its many publications, ASID offers members continuing education opportunities. This means that ASID designers receive the most current information on appropriate materials, technology, building codes, government regulations, health and safety standards, design psychology, and product performance.

An ASID member's appellation may read Jane Doe, ASID; Jane Doe, Allied ASID; or Jane Doe, Associate ASID. Seeing these credentials gives you peace of mind that you've hired someone that cares about professionalism and is continually advancing their education.

For more information on what the ASID appellations mean, visit http://www.asid.org/members/.

DESIGN SUCCESS
U N I V E R S I T Y

Design Success University is a continuing education resource and shortcut for professional interior designers to advance their business and marketing skills. DSU was founded in 2008 by two practicing interior designers, Gail Doby, ASID & Erin Weir.

DSU now serves over 10,000 interior designers in 49 countries with 24/7 education and coaching to show designers how to grow a successful and profitable business.

Gail Doby has a degree in finance and banking and a degree in interior design, and has been working in and around the home furnishings field since 1977, after a 6 year stint in sales and marketing with a Fortune 500 company. She is an NCIDQ-certified, award-winning, published designer. Gail specializes in high-end residential renovation and new construction design and has done projects across the United States since 1987. She is an author and international speaker on business and marketing.

Erin Weir joined Gail in 2005 as an intern after graduating with a four-year interior design degree from Colorado State University. Erin is now the strategic vision director for Design Success University and manages the operations for DSU which is an entirely virtual, global team dedicated to supporting interior design professionals.

Stephen Pararo, ASID/Photos courtesy of Pineapple House Interior Design

CHAPTER 17

RESOURCES AND SPONSORS

LIST OF ACRONYMS

Interior designers, like other professionals, have their own "shorthand" for communicating among themselves and with others in the building industry. The following is a list of the acronyms used in this book.

ASID

American Society of Interior Designers – A professional association for interior designers. Designers must meet certain requirements of education and experience to be granted membership, and must pass the national qualifying examination to advance to professional membership status.

CAD

Computer-aided Design – the use of computer software to produce design drawings, floor plans, elevations, etc.

CAPS

Certified Aging-in-place Specialist – a certification awarded by the National Home Builders Association (NHBA) to builders and interior designers who have completed a course of study on design and building solutions for aging and accessibility.

CFA

Cutting for Approval – cutting taken from the actual bolt of fabric to be used in a project, used to check the quality and color, which may vary by dye lot.

DSA

Designer Society of America – an association for decorators, residential interior designers, space planners, kitchen and bath designers, re-designers; it offers continuing education and a home-study certification program.

DSU

Design Success University – a continuing education resource and shortcut for professional interior designers to advance their business and marketing skills.

GC

General Contractor – responsible for the day-to-day oversight of a project, management of vendors and tradespeople, and communication with the parties involved (e.g., client, designer, architect, etc.). The general contractor hires and manages specialized subcontractors to perform various parts of the work (e.g., plumber, electrician, flooring installer, lighting specialist, etc.).

LEED

Leadership in Energy and Environmental Design – a standard for green building design developed and managed by the U.S. Green Building Council (USGBC).

MDF

Medium-density Fiberboard Construction – an engineered wood product constructed from wood fibers glued together under heat; it is used in furniture, cabinets, doors and wall paneling, as well other building materials.

NCIDQ

National Council for Interior Design Qualification – An independent, nonprofit organization that administers the national qualifying examination for interior designers. In some states, designers must pass the NCIDQ exam and receive their NCIDQ certificate in order to be licensed as a registered or certified interior designer.

NKBA

National Kitchen and Bath Association – a professional association for the kitchen and bath design industry; it provides continuing education and a variety of certifications, including Certified Kitchen Designer (CKD) and Certified Bath Designer (CBD).

DESIGN APPS

Whether you choose to do your project yourself or work with a designer, the following apps will help you get organized and begin narrowing down your choices. In addition, if you are looking for inspiration, there are dozens of design photo, magazine and website apps that let you view pictures of professional projects.

Color Capture® by Benjamin Moore® and ColorSnap® by Sherwin-Williams® can help you find that "just the right color" you are looking for. Use your smartphone to capture a color-rich photo, such as the pattern on a favorite pillow or wallpaper, and these apps for the iPhone and Android™ will scan a multitude of paint hues to find the perfect match.

Handy Man DIY provides the information you need to get your do-it-yourself project done, including videos and a pre-selected materials list for common household projects, shopping lists and task lists. Calculate room dimensions and other measurements and store for later. Estimate costs by entering quantity and pricing information.

Home Interior Layout Designer helps prevent measurement disasters. Set a room's square footage in the app; then enter the dimensions of the item you want to test. You can drag it around the room to see where it fits best.

iHandy Level acts as a level on your smartphone. Indispensable for hanging pictures, etc.

Magic Plan measures your rooms and draws your floor plan just by taking pictures. You can then get your floor plan in PDF, JPG and DXF format or publish an interactive floor plan on the web.

Moodboard is a customizable bulletin board for organizing things that inspire you—images, photos, color swatches, text and more. Share your board with others. It also includes a color palette picker and color loupe.

Peppermint takes the guess work out of choosing colors. It uses a unique

Natural Color System® color wheel to help in selecting analogous, complementary and monochromatic colors.

Photo Measures Lite lets you draw measurements directly on an image you take with your device and save it. It also includes zoom and magnifying features to increase accuracy.

uDecore allows you to visualize photorealistic 3D furniture models and home design items in your room using a photo of the room or your camera's live preview mode. You can customize the appearance to the color and style you like and position items in the room, to see how it will look.

Kristin Drohan's interior design clients asked for a specific combination of comfortable, stylish, durable and eco-friendly furnishings, and not finding a resource that offered those specific benefits, Kristin created a new collection to answer those requests.

Each Kristin Drohan Collection creation has a specific function that is inspired by classic design. The manufacturing process is environmentally friendly and healthy to the consumer.

The Kristin Drohan Collection is made in Hickory, NC, using the highest industry standards:

- Sustainably-forested, kiln-dried or reclaimed wood frames minimize the impact on the environment.

- Corners and other high stress areas are reinforced with corner blocks that are glued and screwed into place for long-lasting performance.

- Heavy gauge spring coils from recycled metal are eight-way hand-tied and nailed to the frame for durability.

- Luxurious seat cushions use three-inch spring coils that reduce sag and cushion breakdown so your furniture looks beautiful even after heavy use.

- A state-of-the-art blend of micro-down in the back cushions provides comfort that quickly bounces back to maintain the beauty of the design.

Your personalized design style can be achieved with your selection of wood finishes, nail head trim applications, dressmaker details, sumptuous fabrics, and size options.

This unique upscale boutique collection is available through your interior design professional. KDC has been showcased internationally in *Mix Magazine*, the *Wall Street Journal*, CNBC, *New York Spaces*, *New England Home*, *JustLuxe*, *New England Finery*, *Interior Living Trends*, and is regularly featured on One Kings Lane®.

NEW ACCOUNT APPLICATION FORM

The Kristin Drohan Collection is pleased to offer a special pricing program to eligible trade accounts.

To qualify, please complete the application form below providing the necessary credentials as requested.

Once completed, please FAX to: (978) 405-5009, attention: Kristin Drohan or if you prefer, scan and email to: kristin@kristindrohancollection.com

PROGRAM QUALIFICATIONS:

Applicants must submit the following credentials:
- Business license or sales & use tax permit
- Proof of membership in one of the following organizations: ASID, IIDA, AIA, IDS, or CID (or have certification of a design degree)

Date of Application: _____ Signature of Applicant: _____

Name of Owner: _____

Company Name: _____

Website: _____

Mailing Address: _____

City: _____ State: _____ Zip: _____

Business Phone: _____ Cell: _____ Fax: _____

E-mail Address: (required): _____

Thank you for your completed application.

We will contact you regarding your acceptance into our program. Note: This is not a credit application.

THE KRISTIN DROHAN COLLECTION
712 MAIN STREET
CONCORD, MA 01742
PHONE: (978) 254-5868
FAX: (978) 405-5009
www.kristindrohancollection.com

To purchase multiple copies of **How To Design Your Perfect Interior** for marketing and gifts contact us by emailing us at info@designsuccessu.com

CPSIA information can be obtained at www.ICGtesting.com
Printed in the USA
LVOW01s1919031013

355342LV00005B/7/P

9 780615 770246